REMEMBERING
THE HOLOCAUST

★

D0613632

MICHAEL E. STEVENS
Editor

ELLEN D. GOLDLUST-GINGRICH
Assistant Editor

Wisconsin Historical Society Press

LIBRARY OF CONGRESS CATALOGING-IN-PUBLICATION DATA
Remembering the Holocaust. (Voices of the Wisconsin Past.)
Michael E. Stevens, editor.
Ellen D. Goldlust-Gingrich, assistant editor.
Includes index.

ISBN 0-87020-293-6 [paperbound]

1. Holocaust, Jewish (1939–1945)—Personal narratives.
2. Holocaust survivors—Wisconsin—Interviews.
3. Refugees, Jewish—Wisconsin—Interviews.
4. Jews, German—Wisconsin—Interviews.
I. Stevens, Michael E.
II. Goldlust-Gingrich, Ellen D.
III. Series.

F590.J5R46   97-16191
1997940.53'18—dc21   CIP
                                                       r97

Front cover illustration: Photo by Claudio Piatto

Contents

Introduction

For all its vaunted progress, the twentieth century has seen more than its share of horror and misery. Indeed, one of the darkest chapters in human history occurred during World War II: the murder of 6 million Jews—two-thirds of Europe's Jewish population—by Nazi Germany in what has come to be known as the Holocaust. Contemplating such a number overwhelms the mind, yet to hear the stories of individual survivors may be even more harrowing, since they assign names and faces to what might otherwise be an abstract reckoning of inhumanity. Ironically, despite their graphic accounts of hardship and terror, the survivors' stories are testaments to hope. By outliving Hitler and the Nazi death machine, the survivors conquered an ideology that sought to destroy an entire people simply because of their ethnic origins or religious creed.

This volume contains some of the recollections of Holocaust survivors who emigrated to Wisconsin immediately before or after World War II. As part of the *Voices of the Wisconsin Past* series, which presents first-person narratives about our common past from the vantage point of the participants, the texts emphasize the lives of ordinary citizens and offer accounts unmediated by the historian's narrative. They provide readers with a sense of the authentic voice of the participants in historic events. The accounts printed here are taken from a remarkable collection of interviews that resulted from the determined efforts of project staff at the State Historical Society of Wisconsin to ensure that the memories of the state's Holocaust survivors were not lost. The first interview, recorded in 1974 at the initiative of the daughter of a survivor living in the Green Bay area, became a heavily used collection at the Society and sparked fundraising efforts for a statewide project in the mid-1970s.

With funding from the Wisconsin Humanities Committee and numerous private donors, the Wisconsin Survivors of the Holocaust project began in late 1979. Sara Leuchter, Jean Loeb Lettofsky, and David Mandel served as the project's staff. Leuchter and Lettofsky recorded 160 hours of interviews with twenty-four survivors living in ten Wisconsin cities. Since the completion of the project, their interviews have been available in the Society's archives on audiotape, and researchers have been aided in finding their way through the materials by a published guide (Sara Leuchter, ed., *Guide to Wisconsin Survivors of the Holocaust: A Documentation Project of the Wisconsin Jewish Archives* [Madison, 1983]). Although researchers could travel to the Society or one of its area research centers to hear the powerful testimonies recorded in the collection, the stories have not previously been available to a larger audience. By printing selections from the interviews, this volume presents multiple accounts of the Holocaust through the survivors' eyes.

The number of Holocaust survivors who moved to Wisconsin is hard to determine. Some scholars estimate the total number of survivors who settled in the United States to be about 140,000. Milwaukee's and Madison's Jewish communities took the lead in state efforts to resettle survivors, although survivors could—and still can—be found in many other communities. The Milwaukee Jewish Family Services, an organization that handled the resettlement of refugees, reported that 150 European Jews came to Milwaukee in the 1930s and an additional 550 came between 1948 and 1950. Rabbi Manfred Swarsensky, who coordinated resettlement in Madison, recalled that twenty-four families came to that city in the postwar period. Thus, it seems reasonable to estimate that between 1,000 and 2,000 survivors came to Wisconsin.

The interviews that appear here have been selected to reflect a variety of Holocaust experiences. By their very nature, memoirs of Holocaust survivors, written or oral, are not representative in any statistical sense. They offer accounts of those who survived the war because of their youth, health, or luck. Furthermore, the interviews took place thirty-five years after the close of World War II, and the interviewees ranged in age at that time from forty-five to seventy-three. The narratives come from persons who were in their teens, twenties, or thirties during the war.

As a genre, oral history has a number of strengths and weaknesses. Because the interviews took place so many years after the described events, there is a danger of lost precision and detail, although many narrators offer remarkably full and minute accounts of events. Furthermore, such recollections normally do not have the narrative structure and clarity of form usually found in written works composed for publication. These shortcomings, however, are offset by the gain in emotional depth offered by first-person accounts. Furthermore, while some of the narrators have written and published their memoirs, many of the interviews here record the stories of individuals who because of their education or personal inclination are unlikely to write memoirs.

The horrors of Nazi concentration camps have been widely publicized in recent years through films, books, and photographs. As a result, there is a tendency to homogenize experiences and assume that all European Jews came from the same social and cultural backgrounds or experienced the Holocaust in the same manner. There also is the danger of remembering those who suffered primarily in their role as victims rather than as individuals with their own unique stories and richly varied cultures.

The selections in this volume have been chosen to counter these tendencies, and the accounts have been grouped by region of origin. The interviews illustrate the range of experiences of European Jews: in Holland, for example, Jews were integrated into the nation's educated professional classes, whereas in Poland and Lithuania there was a long tradition of anti-Semitism prior to the Nazi occupation. Likewise, the survivors of Auschwitz and Dachau tell very different stories from those who experienced the milder conditions of the camps in Italy. The narratives include recollections of the Jewish ghettos of Poland and Lithuania, life while hiding from the Nazis in attics and false closets in the Netherlands, and the comparatively peaceful childhood of an Austrian exile in Shanghai, China. The volume also includes accounts of survivors from Czechoslovakia and Romania who lived under Hungarian occupation as well as one from a Greek survivor. The interviews show the ways in which the war disrupted and forever changed the lives of the narrators. Yet despite their differences, these men and women tell stories of triumph because each survivor defeated the Nazi dream of annihilation.

*   *   *   *   *

Transcripts of the oral interviews form the basis of the material printed here. We have tried to create a clean, readable text without sacrificing the original language of the interview. Because written English differs from spoken English, we employed a number of conventions to deal with variations. We did not change any words or tamper with grammar or sentence structure. Words added to clarify the text always appear in brackets. The transcripts omit false starts as well as filler words such as "you know" or "um." We made no attempt to preserve dialect or pronunciation; the original tapes are available for those interested in these aspects of the interviews. In addition, English was at least a second language (and, in some instances, a third or fourth) for each of the interviewees; in many cases they used Yiddish, German, Polish, or Dutch words in the interviews. English translations appear in brackets after the original wording.

The interviews ranged in length from three hours to nearly twelve hours, and the texts presented here are excerpts. Generally, the text appears in the same order as it did in the interviews, but in some cases, interviewees clarified stories told earlier in an interview and these disparate segments have been moved together. When part of the answer to a question has been deleted, we note it with ellipsis points (. . .), although we have not used them to indicate omissions of entire questions and answers. Questions asked by the interviewers appear in italic type and have been edited for clarity.

*   *   *   *   *

This volume would not be possible without the generosity of the men and women who have agreed to let us print excerpts from their interviews and have given us photographs and other related documentary material. This book is their story. We owe a debt of gratitude to the staff of the Wisconsin Survivors of the Holocaust project—Sara Leuchter Wilkins, Jean Loeb Lettofsky, and David Mandel—who gathered the materials upon which this volume is based. We also thank Charmaine Harbort, who labored long and hard on the difficult task of transcribing the interviews; Sean Adams, who assisted with the background research; and University of Wisconsin Professors Pietro Aragno, Valters Nollendorfs, Irving Saposnik, and Jolanda Taylor, who translated foreign phrases. Paul Hass's usual expert editorial advice was essential in our efforts to turn our manuscript into a book. The Wisconsin Society for Jewish Learning generously provided financial assistance to the project, and Kathleen Jendusa, its executive director, has encouraged our efforts to see the book into print.

*   *   *   *   *

The State Historical Society has worked to preserve the record of Wisconsin's history since 1846. Volumes in the *Voices of the Wisconsin Past* series would not be possible without the donation of letters, diaries, and photographs by the state's citizens. Persons wishing to discuss the donation of documentary material are invited to contact the Archives Division at the State Historical Society of Wisconsin, 816 State Street, Madison, WI 53706.

VOICES OF THE WISCONSIN PAST

REMEMBERING
THE HOLOCAUST

1

Germany and Austria

WORLD WAR II began when Germany invaded Poland on September 1, 1939, but the seeds of the Holocaust were planted much earlier. Jews had lived in Germany continuously since the tenth century, and when Adolf Hitler became chancellor on January 30, 1933, the German Jewish population numbered about 550,000 (around 1 percent of the population). Although Jews had been integrated into all aspects of German life, including business, politics, culture, and science, the Nazis immediately began to "Aryanize" Germany. On April 1 an anti-Jewish boycott was initiated, and further anti-Semitic legislation was enacted throughout the 1930s. Jews were excluded from the professions, universities, and public service (1933); deprived of German citizenship (1935); and required to register property and to carry passports marked with a *J* for *Jude* (1938).

After Austria's incorporation into Greater Germany in March, 1938, Austria's population of 185,000 Jews—170,000 of them in Vienna—became subject to Germany's anti-Semitic laws. Eight months later, the events of *Kristallnacht* (the Night of Broken Glass) marked the beginning of real peril for Europe's Jewry. On the night of November 9–10, widespread anti-Jewish rioting occurred in Berlin and in other cities throughout Germany and Austria. The Nazis characterized the unrest as a spontaneous reaction to the November 7 assassination of a German diplomat in Paris by a seventeen-year-old Polish Jew; in reality, the pogroms were organized and initiated by the Nazis. Mobs destroyed hundreds of Jewish homes, businesses, and synagogues.

In the wake of *Kristallnacht*, the German government stepped up its harassment of Jews. The Jewish community was assessed a fine to pay for damage done on *Kristallnacht* and for reparations for the murder of the diplomat, and new legislation expelled all Jews from public schools, confiscated any businesses that remained in Jewish hands, and effectively eliminated Jews from the economy. In addition, 30,000 Jewish men were arrested and held until early 1939.

1

After the events of *Kristallnacht,* German Jews knew that the situation had become perilous, and many of them frantically sought to emigrate. By 1941, some 240,000 Jews remained in Germany/Austria, and only about 30,000 of them survived the war. Manfred Swarsensky and Susanne Hafner Goldfarb were among those who escaped Nazi Germany; Eva Deutschkron was among those who did not.

Manfred Swarsensky

Manfred Erich Swarsensky was born in Marienfliess, Germany, on October 22, 1906, to a rural family whose ancestors had lived in Pomerania for many generations. Between 1925 and 1932 he pursued rabbinical studies at the Hochschule für die Wissenschaft des Judentums in Berlin; simultaneously, he completed a Ph.D. in Semitics at the University of Würzburg. Upon ordination, Swarsensky served in Berlin's large Jewish community, where he spoke out against the Nazis in his sermons.

Could you describe the events of Kristallnacht?

At about two o'clock in the morning of November 9 to 10, the telephone rang and the *shammes* [sexton of the synagogue], Mr. Yacib Ghirer, a Polish Jew who was the resident sexton of the synagogue on Prinzregentenstrasse, called me and shouted on the phone, "Our synagogue is burning." Then I got up, ran to the synagogue, pushed my hat way down on my face so as not to be recognized by anyone, and there I saw German SS troopers pour gasoline into the interior of the building and over the walls and also German firemen stand on the adjoining building so as to prevent that they be burned down. And so they poured water over those buildings so as to keep them cool.

There was a mob around, I don't know how many, shouting "Death to the Jews" and all the other things. Then toward morning I stood there for a while, petrified, not knowing what in the world to do. There was nothing to do, because the policemen had orders not to protect the buildings. Then I ran, closer toward dawn, to the other synagogue, which was not too far, the Fasanenstrasse synagogue, . . . and there I saw the same picture. Three huge domes, and the fire rising from the pews up into the cupolas—a horrible sight. The inside of the synagogue was all marble and therefore it didn't burn. So then I saw that spectacle at the Fasanenstrasse too.

Following that there was perhaps the greatest feeling of depression all over the city and the community, and the poor Jews just didn't know what to do. Everything was disrupted, no communication, nothing. . . . What people did was just roam around through the city, fearing that they

*Fasanenstrasse Synagogue, Berlin, Germany, after Kristallnacht,
November, 1938.*

might be arrested, because outside of Berlin, in smaller communities
and the country, Jews had already been arrested. . . .

During that night not only synagogues, of course, were destroyed, but
also all Jewish business establishments, and therefore the night [was]
named "crystal night," *Kristallnacht,* because the glass panes of all Jewish
shops were absolutely knocked out. There was the clitter and the noise
and the clatter of everything all around. How did the people know [which
stores] were owned by Jews? Simply because, already on April 1, 1933,
there was a first attempt at a boycott, and the Hitler government had
the name *Jude* [Jew] written on the windowpanes. They were later
removed, but for some reason they knew exactly where those places were,
and they were destroyed.

As a curiosity, I may mention that I knew personally a professor, a
staunch Lutheran, by the name of Professor Paul Kahle, who had one
time had lived in Bonn, . . . who was an Orientalist and worked with
graduate students, Jewish students especially, on his Oriental studies.
He wrote many books. He and his wife went out the next morning to
sweep up, deliberately, the debris of some places. He went out with

dustpan and broom, protesting the matter, and to save his life he had to flee to London. . . . There were instances here and there, not in Berlin, to my knowledge, where some Christian custodians helped Jews save Torah scrolls. This did not happen in Berlin. It was quite impossible. . . .

[After *Kristallnacht,*] everybody was looking for cover, where to go, what to do, because rumors had spread that Jews in the provinces had been arrested and taken to concentration camps right during the night. In Berlin it didn't happen during the night, but it happened, not even the next day, on the tenth. But the rumors were all around.

So what people did, many, especially men—they arrested men first— they were looking for hiding places, a friendly non-Jew. In my case, I didn't know absolutely nothing what to do. And another rabbi, Karl Rosenthal, who was the last rabbi of the real Reform synagogue in Germany, . . . came to see me and said, "What are we going to do?" I said, "I don't know. I have no idea." Karl and I did what everybody else did. We couldn't think of a hiding place. We were running around, just leaving the house, because we were afraid they would come to the house.

So we were running around all night. At that time my parents had moved to Berlin from the little place [where] we were born. They were old and also they had to give up the farm and everything else. They were forced to sell it. They never got the money but they turned it over to some Aryan, and so they were living with me—I was unmarried—in a little apartment. So I went to an elderly widowed aunt and stayed with her overnight.

But then I got up in the morning and about ten o'clock when I got home, one or two students I had—girls—were living on that street where I was, in the west section of Berlin. They called me and said they see on the street Gestapo agents, or SS men, I don't know what kind of— uniformed—entering Jewish homes and arresting individuals. One girl shouted, "They're going to come for you now. I can see it from my apartment." So, she was right. Two guys came, knocked on the door, and said, "Get ready." And it was November and of course psychologically I was sort of prepared. My mother was not. She was crying. So, "Get ready." So they gave me two or three minutes to put on my winter coat and my hat, and we went. . . . And then they asked me how I want to get to a city jail, which was not too far. So I said, in my defiant, ridiculous, childish attitude, "I want to walk." Because I wanted the *goyim* [non-Jews] where I was living to see what happened— the two guys, with guns of course, and I in between. They rejected this request, so they walked with me to the streetcar. I noticed some of the neighbors behind their curtains looking what happened. As a matter of fact, one of the gentlemen, a lawyer, not Jewish, said to my mother, "What did your son do? He must have done something." This was of course the thinking—logical. So by streetcar we arrived at this jail and that was a frightening experience because I had never been an inmate of a jail yet. I thought they would absolutely beat me up. They did not do that, but they squeezed me into a dark cell, totally dark. . . . This was in Berlin yet. And in the jail, it was hot like the devil. I had my winter coat on, and there was just no room. I couldn't even take it off. And when I moved I noticed there were other fellows in that cell, too. I remember a dentist from Charlottenburg, whom I still remember, a nice elderly gentleman. We exchanged a few pleasantries or whatever they were, but the most interesting encounter in that jail was Professor Friedlander, who introduced himself like a real German gentleman and asked me my name or whatnot. And the reason I discovered Friedlander—the cell was maybe half of this room in size—was a sentence came to me which I have learned in high school gymnasium many years ago from Horace, namely, "Mente aequa rebus in arduis." . . . I said it only in Latin, just out loud, I don't know why: "Remember that under arduous circumstances retain your equanimity." I said it to myself. I don't know why, it just came out. Whereupon Professor Friedlander completed the whole thing. He was a professor of classics at the University of Berlin, so he knew it and I didn't. We got quite friendly. It's a relief if you find a fellow sufferer. He said, "For me the tragedy is greater than even for you. I am not Jewish." I said, "I fully appreciate this fact." I didn't want to hurt him or censure him or praise him. There was nothing to hurt, censure, or praise. We were all in the same boat. We were back in the bosom of Abraham, and so there we were.

Nothing to eat, nothing to drink—of course, you have no appetite under those circumstances. I mean, you don't even think in those terms. I always expected someone to come in and take us out individually for beating. This did not happen, but in the evening about six o'clock a guy came and took me out. I don't know what happened to the others—"Come along." We went downstairs, we went not far from there, this was near Kurfürstendamm, the best neighborhood. The synagogue was only a few blocks away. They hailed a cab, and at my expense, these two fellows and I—but I don't know who they were.

Were they civilians?

In uniform. They told the guy to drive me down with them, because they had to surrender me to the headquarters of the Gestapo, which I had known, seen, in 1937 when I was censured for my airing anti-Hitler remarks in sermons and in speeches. So I expected only the very, very worst. I knew, of course, every street, every place that we passed by, I had what we call in French the *chutzpah,* which means arrogance. I don't think I would have this arrogance nowadays, but I said to the fellow, "I would like to call my mother." And I knew exactly where there was a public telephone. I seen it in front of me when we passed by, and much to my amazement he said, "Get going." And of course he came along and I telephoned my mother, at least, I mean, what could I say? So I told her, "I'm on the way to this. Good-bye." Period. And when we arrived there, it was night, seven o'clock, maybe, dark. There were, in the courtyard, hundreds and hundreds of Jews all standing at attention, some with little satchels, most of them with nothing. . . .

This was the then headquarters of the Gestapo in Berlin, all the offices, like a jail. It was partly jail, partly administration, partly God knows what. There were places or branches of the Gestapo. One I had never seen—that was the worst, where they murdered people right away. That was in western Berlin. That was infamous, infamous. If a Jew or anybody heard this, this was just the end of it. But [the place where I was] was a little bit more humane, if you can call it that. In other words, they wouldn't murder you there right away. So there we were standing at the moment. And of course searchlights came over. It was lit. We could see. It was like daylight, but it was dark outside. Some people knew me and said, "Rabbi Swarsensky." That made them feel good, which I understand because misery loves company and they thought I had any clout or any influence. I was in the same boat of misery and uncertainty they were.

So there we were standing, I would say close to midnight, in attention, in anticipation of things to come, and they did come. Maybe at 11:00 p.m. or so, huge police trucks arrived and they pushed all of us. We had to jump on those trucks, and we were inside of the trucks. You even could sit down on some, but it was a miserable thing, and since I knew Berlin I knew exactly where we were going, to the northern parts of Berlin, to a concentration camp. They could have taken us elsewhere, too, but this is where they took us, which was about forty or fifty miles outside of Berlin, Oranienburg-Sachsenhausen. . . .

So, while we were driving out on this joy ride, two young fellows, twins, they were the youngest on this trip, they were maybe eighteen. They knew me. I had bar mitzvahed them at the Fasanenstrasse, and they clung and said, "Oh, what is going to happen, Rabbi?" "Well, I don't know either. Let's calm down," et cetera. I knew exactly what was going to happen because I had known, heard—I'd never seen it—about concentration camps years ago. So nothing good. And nothing good came.

We arrived there by midnight and the concentration camp guards, these are real animals. They jumped upon us. I was in my early thirties and most of them, they were young. Most of the people were fifties, sixties, seventies—old people, too—and they pushed them down from the truck and beat us with whips and so on. Many broke their legs—they couldn't jump. Some were old, some had a heart attack. It was a murderous, hellish sight and experience, and the rest of us they drove through the gate of the concentration camp, Oranienburg-Sachsenhausen. Now, when we arrived there, this contingent—and again it was all lit up by searchlights. It was dark, it was windy, it was cold—November—but at the same time you could see to a degree. We could see, for instance, in the rear, it was a huge field. It was an oval-shaped exercise field where you saw in the rear, somewhere vaguely, barracks, only they are little huts, wooden huts. You saw what was very ghastly inside, thousands of people who were all milling around. They came from other parts of the country. They were way out, like ghosts and skeletons moving around. You didn't know where they were going. You could see that they had striped prisoner clothes on, not their own clothes—the striped concentration camp outfits. You couldn't yet see their number on it and their emblem. Everybody, depending on the category to which he belonged, whether he was criminal, not Jewish; whether he was a priest, a Catholic priest; whether he was a gypsy; whether he was a political prisoner; or whether he was a Jew.

We were standing there throughout the entire night but not just standing. The guards just moved around all of us at random, the way they always did it, beat people just at their "pleasure." They tortured people terribly. For instance, there were some sons—I don't know how they identified them—and their elderly fathers. They made in the sight of all of them, sons beat up their fathers. Would you believe it? Yes. . . . They made old people with luggage in their hands run around the whole field. People collapsed, [had] heart attacks. . . . Only the sturdiest and the luckiest [survived]. The luckiest are those who were not beaten up to death. I got beaten by about virtually everybody, but not so fatally. They hit you with their rifle butt over the head. There's just nothing you can do about it. If he hits you over the shoulder or on the back or otherwise, you survive. So they did this.

The concentration camp is surrounded by huge walls, the inside of which is surrounded by electrified barbed wire. The top also has barbed wire on it and all kinds of glass, broken glass, so you can never get

*Manfred Swarsensky
shortly after his release
from Sachsenhausen,
Germany, ca. 1939.*

WHi(X3)39362

across, plus there are watchtowers, which are manned twenty-four hours
by guards, again with machine guns always directed at the inside. Each
time I pass Waupun and look at the [maximum security prison], which
of course is a summer resort as compared to a concentration camp, but
the sight is a little similar, high walls with guard towers and all the rest.
Now, part of the purpose of the electrified wire is, of course, to encourage
people to touch them and commit suicide. But relatively few people,
in fact very few people, amazingly, would do that and commit suicide,
because—this, I think, is the positive aspect of this—everyone, including
this speaker, had absolute hope that we would get out again. Maybe that's
a Jewish quality. How, I didn't know. I had no idea how ever to get out
again, but I had a feeling this is not the end. . . .

So then, toward morning, we were, registered, given a number.
Concentration camp people, at least in Sachsenhausen, were not tattooed.
Others had a number burned in; we were not [tattooed]. Maybe there were
too many, maybe they didn't have time. They took away everything we
had, gave us a thin pajama, which was just marvelous on the cold winter
nights and days. The only things you kept were your socks and your
shoes, plus they shaved your head. The purpose of it is to humiliate you,
to dehumanize you, so everybody looked like his own skeleton, et cetera.

And then of course the routine of the day began. The routine consisted
seven days a week of the same torture—namely, you slept in barracks.
Now, the barracks, it sounds very elegant, [but] they were just four walls
and a roof, wooden, which was probably built by previous prisoners,
and there was no inside. In other words, you slept on the cold, soggy,
wet ground. There were no mattresses, no pillows, no nothing, but you
slept there with your clothes on, dirty to the *n*th degree, not shaving,
not nothing, packed like sardines. You simply couldn't sleep. It was too
narrow. The guy next to you was snoring, was carrying on. Some were
crying, whimpering, this. It was like in the *gehennom* [hell]. And with
this you were tired, naturally, the next morning, and you were always
tired. I mean, you could never relax or rest, there was just nothing. Not
only that, during the night, fellows came and inspected us to see, with
searchlights, with flashlights, whether we were still around and if
somebody would wake up or look at the guy he would hit him over the
head with a whip. . . .

I was called in one day, out of the blue sky, to appear before the
commander, and I feared the worst, of course. So he called me in, and
when they call you in they never talk to you face-to-face, you don't sit
down. You have to face the wall and he talks. Always you face the wall
and he talks somewhere out of the corner—another method of
humiliation. And then he, shouting of course, nothing civil, [asked]
whether I want to be discharged. Why he called me in, I do not know
to this very day. . . . The guy said under certain conditions, the main
one of which was to leave the country immediately, I could be discharged.

Now comes something which borders on insanity. Nowadays I would
have a different attitude. Anyway, I said no. This, I say, is insanity. It
is not heroism. I don't know, it was foolhardiness of the first order, but
I did feel—and when I say this, this makes me feel better than I am or
was—I just felt I couldn't accept a certain privilege or an exception for
myself which was not given to other Jews because I was a rabbi and
regarded as such we had to keep it from the Gestapo fellows. They were
terrible. They always asked a person what he was, called every Jew a
millionaire. For me, somebody had told the other rabbi, "Tell them you
are a teacher." That was so innocuous. So I said no. The guy gave me
a kick in the pants and out I was. Later on, I don't know how much
later, a miracle. I was called again. . . . [I was having heart trouble,
and] I had a feeling that I would absolutely die if I had to stay in there
longer, so, when they placed the proposition before me again, I said
yes. Because one of the reasons why I was so daring or whatever or
foolish was I wasn't married. I suppose a married person might react

differently. But then I thought for my parents, I thought "What good does it do? If I die here, nobody is helped either." So I gave up my heroism, which was not too deep in the first place, and I said yes.

They made me sign maybe twelve, fifteen statements. Only the first several I could read, just sign my name. They were all matters of form, apparently—forms. First one I remember, that I went into the concentration camp on my own volition, so as to protect myself *von der kochenden deutschen Volksseele,* from the burning, boiling soul of the German people. I signed my name. Another, that I would leave the country immediately. Another one, that I would never talk about the concentration camp anywhere in the world or Germany. The other, the following, I cannot remember. I never read them, I just signed them, because they wanted to get me out. And when I was discharged and escorted to the very exit of this tremendous field and left there alone in the wilderness, a guy addressed me and said that I should remember that the arm—and these are almost quotes, these are words I am not making up—that the arm of the Gestapo is long enough to catch me wherever I am and I will be caught if I ever say one word about concentration camps.

And this fear in me accompanied me for a long time. When I came to this country anywhere I was asked, and I remember the little towns where they have the minister, this and that, to talk about Germany, I always asked the minister "If you want to announce it, always give me a different name." He always called me Dr. Baum, that was my name. Dr. Baum is going to speak. Because I had my parents living in Germany, and it was known that Gestapo spies probably were not in every little Wisconsin town, but they were around, and it was very dangerous in those early years when I was here because they would accuse Jews of spreading *Greulnachrichten,* that means all kinds of cruel, untrue stories just to whip up the sentiments of people against Germany.

Swarsensky continued ministering to the Berlin Jewish community for another month, during which time the Gestapo repeatedly warned him to leave the country. He departed in March, 1939, and, after spending several months in Holland and England, came to the United States in July, 1939.

Tell me about your arrival on Ellis Island.

The immigration officer, when we landed—on Shabbas, Friday afternoon—did not believe me that I was a rabbi, whereupon they put me for several days in the jail in Ellis Island. Now the jail, of course, was summer resort. In the first place, there were hundreds if not thousands of people. I had never seen a colored person in my life. It was the first time I saw colored people, but I saw all kinds of nationality groups, men and women, I never laid my eye on [before]. I was never in Asia, et cetera. They were all detained and I was one of the many. I didn't see a person of my background, not one. I was the only one. . . .

The danger was [that] they could send you back if you were not there legally. The matter was not clear, they could send you back. This was a fear I had. There was nothing I could do since it was a weekend. I knew I had to appear the next day or whenever before a judge. There is a judge, a court, on the island. And naturally I heard the term Ellis Island, but I had no conception of what it was like. I enjoyed myself as best as I could. I read all kinds of pamphlets and I was pushed into the kosher section. I always had to eat kosher, on a compulsion in my life, and this kosher section served, normally I forget, but they had white bread of the American variety, which I had never eaten nor have I learned to like to this day. It always tasted to me like cotton. And then they had what we call peanut butter, which I had never countenanced nor liked to this day. But I ate, white bread, butter, there were pieces of cheese and tremendous amounts of slices of large onions, and I have never eaten or seen anybody eat such big onions. But this was my introduction to the American cuisine.

Came the following week, I was called. I should mention also I was sleeping not in barracks but in huge halls like in Waupun, and everyone gets a little mattress, and it was hot, beastly hot, absolutely. No air conditioning and there were all kinds of characters sleeping left and right of me, and I must admit that I brought to this country . . . oh, I don't know, thirty dollars in my pocket, which appeared to me like a million. And I didn't undress and take the pants off but slept with my right hand in my pocket because one of these characters he looked a little strange to me. I thought he would counterfeit and then I would be totally denuded, et cetera.

And so then I appeared before the judge, who was stern, to the point, but friendly. . . . The guy started asking me all kinds of questions about my rabbinical training. He didn't want to believe me, neither did the immigration officer on the boat. This was off the boat already. I didn't look like a rabbi. Because there were others on the boat *mit langem Kapotes, einem bord, und einem Hütchen* [with long frock coats, their beards, and their small hats], and Swarsensky appeared to be a non-Jew, et cetera. That's the reason he really didn't want to let me in. But this fellow didn't go by appearance but by credentials. So among the things that I had indeed in my little briefcase were rabbinical whatever, testimony from the Hochschule and also some sort of statement from the Jewish community in Berlin that I was a rabbi there. . . .

There was America for me, and I didn't know left and I didn't know right and I didn't know good from evil. I knew nothing. I was reborn, period.

Swarsensky briefly lived with his brother in Chicago before moving to Madison, Wisconsin, in February, 1940, where he served as the rabbi at Temple Beth El, a newly organized Reform congregation. He held that position until his retirement in July, 1976, and took an active role in the city's civic, religious, and social welfare organizations. He was the motivating force behind Madison's program to settle Jewish Holocaust survivors. In 1952 he married Ida Weiner of Chicago, and the couple had two children. Rabbi Swarsensky died on November 10, 1981, the forty-third anniversary of *Kristallnacht.*

*   *   *   *   *

Eva Lauffer Deutschkron

Eva Lauffer was born in Posen, Germany (now Poznan, Poland), on November 12, 1918, to a widowed mother who remarried in the early 1920s, moved the family to Berlin, and established a retail clothing business. Terrified by *Kristallnacht,* Eva's family unsuccessfully attempted to leave Germany. Unable to obtain papers from the U.S. consulate in Berlin, her mother and stepfather attempted to reach Cuba on the *Orinoco* in May, 1939, but Cuban authorities refused to allow the ship to dock, and they were forced to return to Germany.

On May 4, 1939, Eva married Martin Deutschkron. While he worked as a tailor, she performed forced labor for the Siemens munitions factory. In October, 1942, Nazi roundups captured Eva's sister and Martin's parents. In January, 1943, Eva's parents advised the couple to go into hiding.

When did you go into hiding?

One day Martin came home, I was doing forced labor at Siemens, and Martin had delivered a suit—he was doing his tailoring at home—to the man he was working for. We had an apartment, . . . and our janitor was against Hitler. And they had come to our janitor and asked where the Deutschkrons lived, and she had told them on the fourth floor. And they usually had a passkey to all apartments, [but] they couldn't get into our apartment. My husband had a security lock and everything he had locked, and so they were sitting in the hall and our janitor went upstairs and asked, "Why are you sitting here?" "We are here to pick up the Deutschkrons." So she went back downstairs, acted as if nothing was

*Martin and Eva
Deutschkron, Berlin,
Germany, 1942.*

WHi3187/DKN/1/2

[wrong], and she watched for my husband to come home. He came home
[as] she was coming down the stairs from talking to them, and with her
hands she motioned that he should go back, shouldn't go upstairs, and
she took him into her apartment and told him that they are upstairs to
pick us up.

So he went then to my parents and told my parents that the Gestapo
is there to take us, and they said, "Let's see that we get Eva, that she
doesn't get into their hands." My husband took off his Jewish star and
went to the factory, into Gartenfeld, where I worked, to Siemens, and
stood outside waiting for me where we were taken to work like prisoners.

How could he stand there without being detected?

There were many people picking up people, the shift change was
[occurring]. He didn't look Jewish. So then I came from work, and I
of course had the star on, and I saw him standing there without a star.
I knew something was wrong, because you had to have [a] special permit
to use the train as a Jew, and if you lived farther than seven miles away

you got a permit to ride the train, but only from and to work. So I had this permit; he didn't have it. So he couldn't, with a Jewish star, get on the train to come. So when he was there without the star, we never talked. I couldn't go up to him because I would have given him away.

So I got on the train and he got on the same train and we rode back and at the railroad station there was my mother standing, a little farther over at the corner there was my father standing. They were so afraid—if one would miss me, the other one would see me. . . . We all went then to my parents' apartment to decide what to do now. My sister had been taken away already for almost six months—by this time you realize what was going on. So my parents said, "At least stay with us, and let us stay together, and that's good. When they come, we go together." So it was decided then and then we slept one night together and the next morning my parents got up and said, "You are young. You go out and fight for your life. You have nothing to lose. They take you now, you get killed. If they catch you, you get killed, too, but at least don't go without a fight." So we said, "Where should we go? We have nobody."

We had a doctor that was in a mixed marriage and was very nice, so my parents suggested, "Why don't you go to see this doctor? Maybe he knows somebody." And my husband had a cousin—his father's cousin—that was in a mixed marriage and we knew some other people [who] were against Hitler. So we had taken our star off and we're going around to see who would give us shelter, who would help us in any way. So I went to the doctor and . . . he knew of a woman, who turned out to be his mistress, that had a child and her husband was an SS man and was in military service. He got me shelter there to be the maid, to take care of the child so the woman would be free and could spend time with him, which I found out later as I lived there.

And Martin wandered through the streets to see where he could find shelter and he went to his cousin, [Erich Deutschkron], and his cousin said, . . . "We'll take you, but we have the same name, Deutschkron—it's very dangerous, but we won't let you down." So he spent a night or two there and then he walked along the street and a fellow saw him that he had worked with, . . . a fellow by the name of Franz Gomber, who was, I think, Hungarian. He saw him walking down the street. He ran down, because Martin had no star on, says, "Martin you are alive. You are here. What are you doing? Come up and talk to me." So Martin went up and told him, "I am looking for a place to stay. I don't know what to do. Eva is staying there with a woman." This Franz Gomber needed tailors so he says, "I give you a job. You can work here, and you can sleep here on the ironing table, if you want to be satisfied with this and be here." Martin was thrilled to have a place where he could be and earn a few dollars. I don't recall how we made out to stay in contact, Martin and I. I'm sure he had the telephone number from where I was.

I eventually moved completely [into the tailor shop with Martin] and produced from morning to night these jackets and helped with other chores around. At night we would have a little heating plate where we would make a water soup.

Was Gomber Jewish?

He was not Jewish, but he was against Hitler, too, of course, and [with] the money that Martin earned, this Franz Gomber would see that he got [on the] black market some food for us. He would use his money for our survival. Things were going pretty nice, because we were not hungry, too much anyway, we had sufficient to eat. . . .

Somebody saw that there was at night a heating plate, the flame of that little plate, and he came to Franz Gomber and said, "You are hiding somebody there." This fellow was half Jewish, Isaaksohn was his name. He was brought up as a gentile but even with the name Isaaksohn he was living quite legally. And he says, "You are hiding somebody here, Franz, and who are these people?" They had seen us around, they had seen me around, so I guess he trusted him and he told him, "Yes, I'm hiding a Jewish couple." He says, "This man has to get papers. He has to get out. If he stays all the time in this room, he can't survive."

So he was friendly?

Yes. So he said, "If you make me a suit, Martin, I'll get you papers." So Martin made him a suit and he brought him a military paper of a man that got killed in the war. . . . They changed the picture on the papers for Martin and Martin became Franz Erich Gebhardt. And I had a different name, too. Then Martin had this military paper from him and everything went fine. . . .

After we had left our apartment, the Gestapo was there to seal it—we had nothing [with us], because Martin had been to deliver tailoring to his boss and I was doing forced labor, so we just had the clothes we had. We still had contact with [a Gestapo man] and we told him we had nothing—where will we get clothes to change from? He says, "I will go during the night with you in the apartment. I can get the seals, and we will break the seals, and you can grab a blanket or whatever you

*Eva Deutschkron in photo
for use in her false
papers, Berlin,
Germany, 1944.*

WHi3187/DKN/1/4

want to and throw in whatever you can carry. But once you drop
something, if the people underneath will hear that somebody is in the
apartment, it's over—out.''

So we did this just a few days after the Gestapo had sealed the
apartment. Martin stood guard, my parents stood guard, everybody stood
guard again, and during the middle of the night, the Gestapo man and
I went into the apartment. He took a flashlight and I grabbed whatever.
I'd laid out a plan for myself before where I first put a blanket on the
bed and then take things off the hangers and take—I don't remember
what was it important to me to take. But I know I took some clothes
and in my excitement I pulled off a dress and a hanger fell. So that
was the end. We grabbed this blanket with the things and ran. We
somehow had contacted somebody else in the building and they told
us that the people underneath, who were Nazis, had heard that somebody
was in the apartment. But we were lucky enough, we had gotten out.
My mother had given me a very small suitcase, [and] everything we
had fit into that little suitcase. . . .

We made out with my parents to meet once a week, Sunday mornings,
at Martin's father's cousin—[my parents] wanted to see their children,

and we wanted to see them. . . . My parents were picked up [in February, 1943]; they showed up a few Sundays and then they didn't come anymore. So [Martin's cousin] went to my parents' place to see what was going on—he could move around freely—and the apartment was sealed. And I never heard of them again. It was the end of their lives. . . .

[Gomber gambled at night in the tailor shop,] and Martin had to gamble along. . . . One of the [gamblers] that was a Gestapo man became suspicious, and he too came to Gomber and says, "Listen, this Martin that's always here, he is not a gambler." A real gambler knows who's a real gambler, so they saw that he wasn't a real gambler. [Gomber] told [the Gestapo man], and he says that "He's a nice fellow. I'd like to help him. Does he have papers? What does he need?"

Martin had this military paper from Gebhardt, but it needed every three months the new stamp, which Martin didn't have. Fritz Krause was his name. [Martin] showed [Krause] the paper, and he says, "I work in this department, and you come to me and I'll put the legal stamp on it." So Martin says, "How can I go through? There's military control on." He says, "Don't worry. When I tell you, you come to me to the headquarters, you'll come, and you'll be safe." You can imagine how scared he was. He got in fine, Krause put the stamp on it, and Martin had his paper validated.

And this fellow felt very sorry for us and invited us to his house for a good meal. . . . He had potato pancakes, golden brown, fried in butter. We got so violently ill we thought we'd die, because we were undernourished and this fellow meant it so good and gave us these rich pancakes. We didn't know if we'd survive the stomach attacks we had from it. But I've never forgotten him, it was meant so well—how often it can turn against you. But he did a great deed for us by helping us with these papers.

It didn't last very long. . . . I was in the apartment of Gomber with his girlfriend. They had a party and we were doing dishes and cleaning up from the party and all of a sudden I saw men coming in with Gomber and they were opening cabinet doors. And I said to his girlfriend, "There's the Gestapo. You are being searched." Well, what should I do? Where can I disappear? There was no way out. . . . She says, "Just stand there and do your dishes. Just don't worry about it." Which I did—I had no choice, anyway. So they came through and they asked, "Who is this girl there at the sink?" "That's my wife's girlfriend helping her." And they left.

Later I found out they had been at the tailor shop and they asked, "Who is this man sitting on the table?" and he said, "It's my tailor."

"And how many employees do you have?" "One." [Martin] was the only one there, the other one was sick that day. Luck was with us, and they gave Gomber the order to come that afternoon to the Gestapo for more questioning, and Gomber told us that the Gestapo man who had come in was an old, old friend of his [whom] he hadn't seen for many years. So luck was with us all the way around because this man was not eager to catch him. If he would have wanted to catch him, he would have asked for papers, which he didn't. So of course we disappeared and when Gomber went in the afternoon to the Gestapo he said, "Why, I don't know what you want. I have one tailor working, come and look. What's wrong?"

> The Deutschkrons then left Gomber and stayed briefly with Erich
> Deutschkron in Spandau before their hiding place was again betrayed. They
> returned to Berlin, where several families helped to hide them, including the
> Peltzers, who were acquaintances of Martin Deutschkron's father and who
> lived in Borkheide, a suburb just outside the city.

[After the bombing of Berlin intensified in late 1944,] I became frantic. I carried on something terrible. I can't be in Berlin anymore, "Let's go out to Mr. Peltzer's cottage and see what he can do." By this time it had become about October, 1944, and we went out to Borkheide and Mr. Peltzer's house. He knew who we were; his wife and daughter did not know who we were. So we told him, "Why don't you tell your wife that you have people who are frantic and that they should let us just stay for nights there?" We would go in the daytime to Berlin. So he told his wife that Martin is working in Berlin as a tailor—that's why he's not registered—and that we would just sleep on the porch outside.

We slept on the floor on the porch. Everything we had we put on ourselves, and in the daytime we would go out into the woods. In the beginning we took a train into Berlin to Mrs. Heilman, who had gotten tailoring work for us and helped us earn some money this way to buy [on the] black market some food. And at night we had to leave her apartment and then we went out to Borkheide because when it got dark the bombing always started and I was frantic. She didn't want to keep us there anyway out of fear people would see us. . . .

Christmas Eve [1944], we were still commuting into Berlin and we were on our way out to Mr. Peltzer's and a control [a Nazi official who checked people's documents] was in the train. Martin had an eye for the Gestapo, and as the electric train doors closed he says, "Now we've had it. They are in here to control people." And Martin had carried for quite some time in one pocket a little hand grenade, a little cherry grenade, and in the other pocket a gun, and he said, "If they come to get us, we both get killed. I will set off the grenade and by the chance, either the Gestapo men get shot or we get shot. I'll somehow or other try to use the gun. If we get a chance to get away we'll try to, but those are two things—they shall not get us alive." So they were controlling all the people while the train was moving and the train pulled into the railroad station and he was controlling the person sitting next to me. They controlled the person next to me; Martin had his hand on the hand grenade because it was the only thing that he felt would work, the gun wouldn't work. The doors opened and the Gestapo men walked out. We went out to Borkheide and decided that was the last time Martin would go to Berlin. We told them that the situation in Berlin is so bad and that he would do anything they want him to—the war has to be over pretty soon—if he could stay with them. They consented. He did a lot of sewing for them, and they were building a new house for their daughter.

Martin didn't see the outside anymore after this. We had a little bathroom that they gave us then in a new house. The bathtub wasn't in yet, and we slept on the floor in there. And the daytime then they were building a bunker that was [a] shelter in the ground in the woods. They had to get wood, and Martin got himself a hernia at the time by carrying all this heavy wood and digging out the ground. And they put food in there, water in there, and when the bombing would get too bad then we would all run into the woods there and sit in this hole and hope to survive that way.

The women would constantly question me and catch me in lies. I'm a very poor liar. And they would go to Martin and say, "Gebhardt, why is your wife such a liar?" And he would try to get me out of it. . . .

I would go into Berlin by train and promise Martin with all I could that before dusk I would be back out there. I, believe me, wanted to be out because it was just terrible, the bombings in Berlin. I was always at night out there, and in the daytime if I didn't go into Berlin we would stay in the woods and go to farmers or do things, try to get food together for us. . . .

[In May, 1945,] we thought the war was over because the Russians had come in. That night we identified ourselves to the Peltzer family, the wife and the daughter, who we really were, and of course they were overwhelmed hearing our story and realizing what had gone on and they understood some of the lies now and all these things that they had been curious to them.

Were they friendly toward you?

Then they became very friendly. It lasted one night and . . . all of a
sudden the Germans were back. . . . So word came around that the
Germans are back and . . . everybody quick disappear.

What about the Russians?

The front was going back and forth. So at this point we knew we had
to flee. I had never been on a bicycle, there were not enough bicycles.
By this time we had my girlfriend [Miriam Grunwald] out in Borkheide,
too . . . and we had to flee. And, of course, the Peltzer family had to
come with us. By now it was all known—they were proud of it, they
had harbored us.

So they talked?

Yes. We all got on bicycles. . . . I had never ridden a bike, but when
it comes for your life—so I rode, and I ran into everybody and I fell
down how many times. We rode all the way to Gommern and the Elbe,
a hundred kilometers, who knows how many it was. We rode on the
bike up there. Of course, [it] was all under the Germans yet, but it was
such chaos nobody bothered much.
    One time we went into a military control and of course the daughters
and everybody knew we couldn't stand the military control at this point
anymore. Martin's papers were not up to date and sure enough on the
highway this miliary control, and the man got hold of Martin's papers
and was starting to question and Martin had some health papers there
and he said, "So why are you discharged from the military, for health
reasons or something?" and Martin just pointed to his head. And Mr.
Peltzer's daughter got completely hysterical, crying, screaming, yelling,
and carrying on. I was paralyzed, but she carried on so that the Gestapo
man got scared of her, wanted to get rid of her, says, "Get going. Get
out of here." She saved our life at this moment.

But this was spontaneous?

Spontaneous, totally. Because she knew she would be put against the
wall. She was hysterical for herself, not for us.

WHi3187/DKN/1/9

Eva, Edward, and Martin Deutschkron in Central Park,
New York, July, 1947.

You had no official papers?

Yes, without papers. There was no more fighting. There was nothing.
The Americans could have come easy over the Elbe, taken everything
over. There were no German soldiers around anymore. After this
military control there was nothing—it was peace. But there was an
agreement that to stop at the Elbe and the Americans of course stuck
with the agreement, while the Russians had to come up to the Elbe.

So we went for a walk and Mr. Peltzer came up to us and said, "I
want from you a statement that I brought you through the war." And
we said, "We are glad to give you a statement that you helped us get
through the war," because there were many other people that had
actually done much more than he had done for us, and we didn't know
what we owed whom and how we should show our gratitude if we came
to this point. And Mr. Peltzer said, "Let's go in the woods for a walk"
—Miriam, Martin, and me—"and if you don't give me this paper I will
turn you over to the Germans." So we said, "Mr. Peltzer, we have
to be honest. Let's go back and you turn us over." We had somehow
thought either he doesn't have the courage, because if he turns us over
to the Germans, he's in trouble, too, because why does he have us here
on his hands? Or we would run away. I don't know what we had planned

for that moment. And as we walked back into the city, the Russian tanks rolled along the streets. It was May 5, 1945. And Mr. Peltzer became frantic and said to us, "Forget what I said. The war is over." And we said, "Mr. Peltzer, we will forget what you said, but get out of our lives. Right now we are parting paths, and just don't ever enter our lives again. You have helped us. This is fine, for this we leave you off the hook now. But don't enter our lives ever again."

After the Nazi surrender in the spring of 1945, Eva and Martin Deutschkron remained in Berlin, hoping to find surviving relatives. With the help of American soldiers, the Deutschkrons reestablished contact with family in the United States, and they immigrated there in early 1947. Eva's brother had attended the University of Wisconsin in Madison prior to the war, and the Deutschkron family, which grew to include two children, moved there in November, 1948, and established a tailoring and retail clothing business. Martin Deutschkron died in 1985; Eva still lives in Madison.

Many of the people and events from the Deutschkrons' time in hiding are detailed in Peter Wyden's *Stella* (New York, 1992), which tells the story of a Jewish woman and her lover, Rolf Isaaksohn, who collaborated with the Nazis and who at one time betrayed the Deutschkrons.

*   *   *   *   *

Susanne Hafner Goldfarb

Some Jews found refuge from Nazi persecution in Japanese-occupied China. Jews had lived in the port city of Shanghai beginning in the mid-nineteenth century, when between four and five hundred Sephardic Jews from Baghdad settled there and subsequently prospered. In addition, between three and four thousand Russian Jews immigrated to Shanghai between the Bolshevik Revolution of 1917 and the early 1930s. After *Kristallnacht,* Jews began to stream into Shanghai, an open city where people could land without visas or other official documents. Refugees were further aided by Japan's enactment on December 6, 1938, of a policy that allowed the continuation of Jewish immigration to Shanghai. By December, 1941, more than 16,000 European Jews had found a haven there.

These refugees included Susanne Hafner, who was born in Vienna, Austria, on February 17, 1933, the only child in a middle-class Jewish family that fled the Nazi occupation in early 1939. The Hafners—including Susanne's grandmother and several aunts and uncles—settled in Hongkew, a residential district that was declared a restricted Jewish area on February 18, 1943. With the aid of the Sephardic and Russian Jewish communities, the refugees maintained a functioning community that reestablished many of the commercial, religious, cultural, and educational institutions of their native lands. Despite this relative freedom, most refugees eked out a meager living: Susanne's parents delivered bread in the neighborhood. Although the refugees did not suffer unduly under the Japanese occupation, they did experience terror and hardship resulting from the war in the Pacific, particularly in 1945, when Allied bombings of Shanghai became common.

Susanne Hafner on the S.S. Conte Bianco Mano
en route to Shanghai, January, 1939.

What was your daily life like in Shanghai?

We went to school in the afternoon. We played in plays in school, we played volleyball, things like that. We had no toys, so we'd stuff our own dolls and make dolls and make our own dollhouses. Once, my friend, Doris, came over and she looked in this crate which I had made as a dollhouse, my own little private dollhouse, and there was a cockroach and she said, "What's that?" "That's my doll's dog." And it was the most natural [thing].

How did the Japanese treat the refugees?

From my point of view, it wasn't bad, especially in comparison to how people had been treated in Europe by the Nazis. Some of the Japanese behavior was a little irrational. They would yell and they would scream and they would kick and something like that. That was in individual cases, but I do not recall anything terrible. They facilitated our being in school.

What was a typical day for you in Shanghai?

Going to school, that will be a typical day. I have to describe it in winter. My husband doesn't believe that that was the way it was. He said I'm exaggerating. Get up in the morning, it was freezing. That's the first thing I remember, the cold, and I don't know whether the temperatures were that low, but we were cold—icicles on the window. My parents had left already because they would get up at 2:00 in the morning or 2:30 to go. My grandmother would get up before I did and she would heat the wooden stove. And then in order to make coffee or tea or whatever we had—I don't remember—I had to go and get water from the water man. I don't know why we didn't do it at home, but that was the thing. So I had to walk across the street somewhere and pick up hot water. There was a business—hot water. And I'd get hot water, then I'd have my breakfast. My grandmother would prepare it.

What did you have?

Maybe a sandwich. What could we have? There was no milk or anything like that. And then I'd pick up my girlfriend and we'd go to school. And I loved school, I always did. School was fun, competitive, for me at least. I always felt competitive. About three o'clock I'd be home, first thing on order, we did our homework. By that time my parents would be home and then we ate dinner, whatever that was. I just don't remember all the details. And then if I had more homework, I'd do my homework. If I had less I'd go to Betar [a Zionist youth group]. That was our meeting place.

What were the blackouts like?

Fun. Part of it was fun, I mean, until 1945, when the real bombings began. I mean, up until a certain point [the air-raid drills were] all prophylactic, so to speak. We'd hear the bombing in the outskirts and even that was very faint. I don't think we ever really appreciated the danger. But the last year was bad. That's when the real bombings began, and that's when they started bombing the city. And when they came regularly we knew—for instance, around noon, we'd hear the B-52s, B-29s, and that's when we ran to the theaters, [which] became the air-raid shelters.

What did you feel when the bombings got worse?

Fear, because we knew that if we heard the planes they could bomb us anywhere, and we had really no place to run to. We were on the second floor and we'd run down to the first floor and sit on the stoop, and what could you do? And there were some people there. Sometimes it was funny, because there were people there and somebody would scream "Shema Yisrael" [the first line of a Jewish prayer, "Hear O Israel"], and there were people with senses of humor and who would laugh. Then when we heard [the planes] really overhead we would be scared for a little while.

The thing that scared me later on, after the first bomb that fell really within the residential area, was that I always knew that my father and mother were out in the field, so to speak. I never knew where they were and that's when [the bombing] happened. It frightened me. Sure, it was frightening. I mean it would be frightening to anyone at times. . . . I was always very nervous to know where my parents were, and that's always stayed with me. That was the time I started getting very protective and taking on the parental role, as though I could help anyone. Rather than being the child and being taken care of, I was the one who worried.

Do you remember the spectacular bombing raid of July 17, 1945?

That was a big one. That was the turning point. I remember very distinctly. I remember being in school. Our school was next to a Japanese school. Every time we went to school we would see the Japanese kids. Actually, from where I lived we'd hit the Japanese school first and then around the corner is our school. And there was nothing. Just because they were Japanese, I never considered them as enemies. They were kids just like we were.

Just before July 17 [the air raids] started coming more regularly around noon—11:30, 12:00. And the air raids went on and next to the school there was some kind of a radio station with an antenna. I remember seeing it, even. And then [they] would send us home during the air raids because our school was not set up for air raid shelters or anything like that. We'd run home, run, and that was more than a mile.

Now this part about July 17, how that happened, I was on Chusan Road. . . . It was the black market, it was everything of the Jews. I was running along and the air raids were on. I mean, there were several alarms. There were the precautionary alarm and then there was the regular alarm, which meant that they were there. And I was running and I ran into a house and it was just luck and I met my mother in there. She was delivering bread but she had run in, had to get off the street, and all of a sudden we heard the bombs fall. That bomb I will never forget because that was so close, it felt like it was right on top of us and the minute it fell and we walked to the front, people were running already and people were carrying the wounded. And my only thought was where was my father. And then, of course, that same day we found out that it had hit the Jewish quarter by mistake and that several Jewish people were killed. In fact, one of the boys who went to school with me, his mother was [killed]. So this is a personal one I know. And then there was a lot of looting after that because the houses were [damaged]. And after that, whenever there was an air raid, I mean, we knew that it could hit anywhere, and that was frightening. But that started July

WHi(X3)39329

Susanne Hafner (third from right) with family, including her parents, Max and Martha (far right), Shanghai, China, 1946.

17, and don't forget, the war was over in August. So it was the last three weeks.

Did the refugees and the Chinese work together?

Oh, they were very cooperative, yes, yes. I mean, they worked as a unit. The cleaning up and, yes, people worked together. Even the Japanese worked together with us. I mean, the air raid wardens and so on, this was all done in conjunction with the Japanese. We actually had to be on their side.

What was it like when the American rescuers entered?

All of a sudden you would see American soldiers in the streets, but there was no marching in. The mood was good, but there was no overt rejoicing on the street. Again, there was no [celebration] as you would have seen in Paris when soldiers moved in. For us, of course, it meant food, because they brought the rations, the K-rations and the surplus army food.

Then the good period started in a way because the Americans, there would be people coming to schools and some of the soldiers would bring chewing gum and candy and they'd have special parties for us, Hanukkah parties and Simchas Torah parties, and I remember the soldiers being very involved. It was all so strange, to see an American—"Oh, he's Jewish," this kind of thing.

One funny scene I have to tell you is I remember it was Pesach,[1] and this was already quite a while after the war, and there were four rooms on the floor where we lived and one man had left because he had a son in Scotland so as soon as the war was over, he could go to Scotland. So right into that apartment there was a Chinese lady moved in. I call her a lady, but she was a prostitute, a real prostitute. . . . Her name was Josephine, and I'll never forget Josephine because Josephine used to come home at night, we'd hear her come home drunk, couldn't walk, arrive either in a petty cab or in a rickshaw and bring a soldier along. And the next morning the soldier would get up, you'd see him, and here we were kids—we would go, "Hush, hush, hush," and we knew she was a prostitute. And one—this is funny—it was Pesach. We had the doors open, and there was matzo on the table and one of the soldiers

---

[1]Passover, the spring holiday commemorating the exodus of the Jews from Egypt.

came in with her. And he woke up, I think, the next morning, what happened was, he looked and he saw the matzo, and he was Jewish, and he forgot about Josephine and he just walked in with this feeling of being among Jewish people. So I just remember that because it was funny. And poor Josephine was left without him.

The Hafners moved to Israel in early 1949 as part of the Jewish community's mass departure from Shanghai in the wake of the Chinese Communists' accession to power. In August, 1953, the family immigrated to New York City, where Susanne married Stanley Goldfarb in 1963. In 1969 the Goldfarbs moved to Madison, Wisconsin, where Susanne worked for the University of Wisconsin's Office of Foreign Students and Faculty until her death on June 15, 1987.

2

The Netherlands

JEWS had lived in Holland since the late sixteenth century and enjoyed tolerance and security of life and property. At the time of the German occupation in 1940, about 140,000 Jews (including refugees who had fled the Nazis in Germany, Austria, and Czechoslovakia) lived in the Netherlands, constituting 1.6 percent of the country's total population. More than half of all Dutch Jews lived in Amsterdam. On May 10, 1940, Germany invaded the Netherlands. Three days later, Queen Wilhemina fled to Britain, and on May 14 the Dutch army surrendered. The Germans installed a civil administration and permitted the Dutch government to continue to function, though without its leaders, who had fled with the queen. The two administrations worked together throughout the war.

Anti-Jewish policies were implemented in the fall, 1940, when Jewish businesses were required to register with the government and all Jews were suspended from the civil service. A January 10, 1941, decree required anyone with a Jewish grandparent to register. In February, 1941, the Dutch Nazis intensified the anti-Semitic campaign, rounding up a relatively small number of Jews from Amsterdam's Jewish quarter and deporting them to Buchenwald and Mauthausen. As a result of these arrests, a general strike took place in Amsterdam, and the city was shut down for two days until the Nazis quashed the rebellion. In the summer of 1941, the government imposed a curfew on Jews: they could not go out between 8:00 p.m. and 6:00 a.m. and could shop only between 3:00 and 5:00 p.m. In subsequent months, Jews were removed from public schools, barred from public places, and had their property confiscated. On April 29, 1942, Jews were required to wear a yellow star.

The anti-Jewish measures effectively threw many people out of work, and the Dutch and German administrations decided that all unemployed people would be compelled to take up work in Germany, providing the

29

rationale for mass deportations. Beginning in the summer of 1942, men, women, and children were sent first to Westerbork and Vught, concentration camps within the Netherlands; from there, they were transferred to Auschwitz, Sobibór, and other camps in Eastern Europe. Of approximately 107,000 Dutch Jews who were deported, only 5,200 survived the war.

About 25,000 Jews in the Netherlands—the most famous of them being Anne Frank and her family—went into hiding with the aid of the Dutch underground, which was quite active. Roughly two-thirds of the Jews in hiding escaped detection and survived the war, among them Herb DeLevie and his family and Flora Bader.

Herb DeLevie

Born in Rheine (Westphalia), Germany, on May 7, 1934, Herb DeLevie was the second of two children born to a German mother, Hertha, and a Dutch father, Nathan, a prosperous cattle dealer. The DeLevie family, which had roots in Holland dating from the 1600s, moved to Stadskanaal, Holland, in 1936 to escape the growing persecution of Jews in Germany.

Were your parents friendly with non-Jews?

Yes, you would almost have to be. The Jewish community was very small, and our synagogue, which was relatively small, could seat maybe a hundred people in the High Holidays. They would come in from all surrounding towns, small towns, very much like a small village does here in the States. In our town, like I said, we were only three Jewish families, or four.

What was the population of Stadskanaal?

About 8,000. So the entire Jewish community, gathering about seven small towns of equal size, would fill the synagogue, but that would be about it.

Was there anti-Semitism before the war?

Not until about mid-1940s. The Germans invaded Holland in 1940. They did not really start making their presence known in all parts until the middle 1940s. The very first thing I remember is my mother crying and my father saying that he would have to make preparations to go into hiding because he felt that the Jews were going to be gathered like in

WHi(X3)49696

Herb and Edith DeLevie ice skating,
Stadskanaal, Holland, 1940.

Germany and there was no way out. And in the 1940s is when I remember—that exactly I don't recall. I was what, six, seven.

Did your schoolmates tease you?

The Dutch, not at all, no, not before the war. Before the war, in general, the townspeople were very anti-German. Our friends were very pro-Jewish. No, I never felt anything before the war.

> In late 1940, Nathan DeLevie went into hiding; his wife and children joined him six months later. For four years the family hid in one room of a small farmhouse on the outskirts of Stadskanaal together with an uncle, an aunt, three young cousins, an elderly couple, another cousin in his twenties, and several people in transit. To keep occupied, Herb sketched his surroundings and read more than 3,000 books provided by the Dutch underground.

What was it like when you joined your father in hiding?

We arrived at night and we were very excited, and I remember running to say hello to my father and running through the place which was going to be our home, and we knew it was going to be. For how long, we didn't know, but we knew we were going to be there for quite a while. And this house was a very typical farmer's helper-type house. It was one building. We came in the back door; the front door, I guess, was never used. I don't ever remember it being opened. When you walked out the back door, immediately to the right was the outhouse, which was the only toilet in the place, and from there when you walked past, if you made a left turn you walked into a small barn, which contained a horse pen, a pigpen, and two cattle stalls and an opening space large enough to have a little bit of hay and one wagon.

It was a very small farmhouse. That particular barn was on one side of the house, and then if you walked to the back door instead of turning left you went straight ahead you went into the main kitchen, which was also the main living room. It was a combination kitchen and living room, and it had two bedsteads in it. These were big closets that open up and had the built-in beds. From there you walked straight ahead and to the left there was their formal living room, which also housed two bedsteads. That was to be our room. And immediately to the right of that corridor was another bedroom, which was used for the people who lived there. It was a relatively small room. And that was the extent of the house. There was no attic and there was no basement. There was crawl space and the rafters were right up to the ceiling. There was nothing there, just a little typical Dutch farmhouse. Dirt floor in the kitchen and the barn and the room we were in and the front room had a wooden floor with about a foot and a half, two feet of space underneath it when we got there. We made a trap door into that room and made a big hiding place underneath the floor, but that happened while we were there.

Who owned the farm?

A family by the name of Drente. A man, wife, and two daughters. He was a day laborer, very poor. He used to make his living off working on farms for people, seasonal, and running a *bagger* [dredging] ship, which is a flat boat that would mix up turf that you burn for fuel. . . . When I say run, that means you load the boat and the man pulls it with the rope, or you have a horse that pulls it and he drives the horse. You pull this through the canals, which was quite common in Holland. So the family was very poor, the house was a very poor house, very simple, again, very low class, bottom of the scale Dutch type of living.

When did other people join you in hiding at the farmhouse?

My father's brother was the first one to come. The timing, I guess, was about two or three months where my father's brother was in one place and his family was someplace else and they couldn't stay where they were. First, my father's brother's underground contact came to find out if he could be hidden with us, and I recall that being discussed. First he came, and then within a very short time thereafter the rest of the family joined by the wishes of my uncle. Again with the agreement that, okay, a few more doesn't make any difference, it isn't going to last very long anyway. So his wife came with three children. The kids were all within one year of each other up and down. One was one year younger, one was my age, and one was one year older. Two boys and one girl. The girl was the oldest.

Who else joined you?

After they had joined us was an older couple, Dalsines—they were like a second cousin to my dad—joined us. They were considerably older. He had a very bad case of asthma, and he was in his middle fifties, middle to late fifties, and they came and joined us and that was about two months after my uncle did. Then there was a family that lived with us for about four months. That was a temporary—they were only going to be there for a week. It was a man and wife and three children again, and they stayed for about four months before they were moved elsewhere. Then a cousin from my father, a single man, came and joined us. He was about twenty-one, twenty-two, and he stayed for the duration. This gentleman took care of our education when he came. He had a college education, and he was the one who taught us. He stayed for the duration.

How many children were in the house?

At one time there were eleven kids. It was a short time while the family with the three kids were there, another family came in with two kids, and then there were two kids by themselves that came, without parents, for a short period of time. They were there for six weeks, two months.

Did this become a common place for the underground to bring people?

Not really, considering the amount of people that had to be hidden. I'm saying this all as if it happened all at once; it really wasn't so. For about a year, it was just my father's brother and his family and us. Then after about a little less than a year, the old couple joined us. Then for four months then the single man joined us and just about the same time the family with three kids were there for four months. For about two weeks before they left, the two kids came and joined us by themselves, and they were all removed again and put elsewhere. I have no idea what happened to them, just lost track. The nucleus of the group was for about two years the adults, the older couple, the single man, my father's brother and his wife, my parents, and us five kids. Those were permanent residents, so to speak.

And all of these people were living in that one room?

That's right.

How did you deal with so many people in such a small space?

First, it was no problem, of course, even with all the people, because everybody is fresh. Usually when you arrive you have some amount of supplies of some kind, whether it be food, something to read, these type of things. The biggest problem at first was the children, to keep them quiet and from fighting, and you played games and you did odds and ends to keep occupied. So the first five, six months were no problem. Then the little bickering began. Each group as they arrived had a different source of the underground and depending what the source is your supplies would be different. So what everybody got would not necessarily be the same as far as food and clothing or whatever the underground would bring in or be able to bring in. The first six, seven, eight months weren't too bad.

We were told to be absolutely quiet, the children were. My father insisted I learn how to draw and he stood behind me with a stick and made me draw, copy things, whether it be a bird or a building or a tree or draw a cow or whatever it was. And we had sufficient games to amuse ourselves with for the first period of time. Also the first months, not knowing how long it was going to be and having been separated for some time, there was a lot to talk about.

After a while, the talking ceased and the nerves began to set in. The food became more scarce, small illnesses began—small colds—and you couldn't cough so you coughed in a cushion. And privacy became an irritant—going on the potty in the room, people became a little pickier. Everybody became a little more on each other's nerves. One of the main sources of irritation was the older couple that joined us. The gentleman had asthma. He'd be burning something in a little cup that would smell up the whole place and be coughing like to clear your throat and his asthma condition and that would be done in a tent because it had to be kept quiet.

The biggest argument I remember was that after he'd been there about six, seven months he got a couple of eggs from one of his sources and my father felt that the eggs should be cooked—this happened a couple of times—and they would eat the egg, this older couple, and us kids would be watching. And my father was kind of temperamental anyway, so he lost his cool one time and said, "The least you can do is give the kids the egg instead of eating it yourself." And that led to a big argument with the result being that we got, in turn, first was the youngest, which was my cousin, got a little top slice of the white, and he ate that, and the next time there was an egg we all had the rotation. It was this type of a thing that became a very great irritant.

Also, the other kids became very bored. They were not as self-involved, I guess is the word, as I was. I did a lot of reading. There were always plenty of books, and if I'd read them once I'd start over again, and I was drawing and I enjoyed it. None of the others did. This period was all before the single gentleman joined us. After about nine months that we were there, this younger man joined us.

Just before he arrived my aunt had a nervous breakdown and just about the same time that she had a nervous breakdown, the SS decided that there should be a watch at the road that went past the place that we were in hiding, and they set up a permanent watch to check everybody going back and forth there because they decided there was smuggling going on from Germany into Holland. So now we were faced with having two Germans sitting by the back door who often came in for coffee in the one room, and when they were there, of course, we couldn't even as much as whisper. They would sit in the main room, which was the kitchen/dining/living room for the people, and we were in the next room over. It was visible if the door was open and you could see two doors leading from the corridor. Luckily they never really went in because the people we were hiding with were kind to them, so to speak. Also the owner, the man, had gotten a job working for the Germans and the older girl was dating some of the Germans and worked as a secretary for them and they were generally considered by them as being traitors and being supportive of the Germans and against the Dutch. So they were treated by the Germans as more or less special people, which made it a little easier for us because they were not considered a risk anymore.

The first real illness was the nervous breakdown of my aunt, which lasted for almost two or three weeks. I remember her having to be tied to the bed because she wanted to move around and wanted to get out and my mother and her husband and my father putting a pillow over her head so nobody would hear her screaming and so on. Right after that my sister had a nervous breakdown, wanted to get out, wanted to kill herself, and while she was having that, the oldest girl of my father's brother ended up with the measles and that became the biggest fear, fear of the different sicknesses and how to treat it because there was just nobody you could call in so you did the best you can. Luckily things worked out.

But these things added that much pressure to it at the same time the food became scarcer. It was harder and harder for the underground to come in and supply on a regular basis, and of course the people who were hiding us could not go in and purchase sufficient food to feed that many people without [people] asking questions. So we basically at that time started and continued to have a steady diet of brown beans with no meat and water, and that lasted for just about the duration. Occasionally we had a little piece of *spek,* which is pork fat. And when I say little piece, it would be about a centimeter square and we'd work on that little tidbit at a time.

After we were there about nine, ten months, just about when my sister was so bad, this single gentleman joined us, and there was a lot of discussion as to whether we wanted him or not and it was decided that we would take him in because he was more educated. He was a second cousin of my father, and he would then educate us and keep us busier with schoolwork, which is the way it worked out to begin with. However, at first he slept on the floor like everybody else, but he got close to the [Drentes'] oldest daughter and ended up sleeping with her. . . . After he'd been there for about four months he started sleeping with her and nine months later she had a baby, which everybody said was an SS baby, but this caused some additional crises because now this young man was living more or less with the family and eating better and sleeping better than the rest of us. He was still teaching us, but now he was treated more or less as the husband of the older daughter. During that entire thing, the discussions that went on about this, the arguments, the discussions or fights my father and his brother had with this fellow, Benny, were very severe from the standpoint of "How can you do this at times like this, number 1. Number 2, you're Jewish, she's just a *shiksa* [non-Jewish girl], how can you? You lower yourself." You know, "What about your parents' memories," et cetera.

Just before the baby was born my mother came down with a nervous breakdown, and that lasted for about thirty days. In between that time the Dalsines, the older couple, were offended by the different problems we would have and the older man was feeling kind of sickly but they had gotten to the point that they would just sit in a corner and hang a sheet around them and didn't want anybody to approach them. That was their corner, they wouldn't talk with anybody, they wouldn't share with anybody. They'd get books to read—they wouldn't share. They got very impatient with the kids and apparently we got on their nerves like they did on everybody else's nerves, and they would begin to hit out at us and then my father would get back at them and it got to be a very stilted free-for-all. That was the general atmosphere, and it pretty well continued. Every adult during those three years was ill and three of the children. I myself stayed healthy and so did my oldest cousin.

Occasionally there were notifications, just about once a month, every six weeks, of house-to-house searches and depending on how or who was conducting these, we would either hide underneath the floor in a hiding place that we had dug out or go out in the field at night and hide out there and sometimes we were out there for four or five days not knowing when [we would be able to go back].

Did the Drentes bring you food at night?

No, there was no way to do that because we had to sneak out when the Germans were either being kept occupied or would not be there for a short period of time and then they would reappear and we'd have to wait until they leave. At one time we were out there I think for twenty-two days. This was during the fall and we ate the corn that was there and grass and whatever we could find, drank the water that was running through the little moats that are very plentiful in Holland. Actually, there was never a house search at this place, so even though we took the precautions, as it turned out, the house was never searched. Once somebody came in and when they recognized that [Mr. Drente] was working for the SS, they just said, "Well, how are you?" and had a cup of coffee and left.

The day-to-day stories are pretty much a repeat of the generalization. I can't remember all the little fights and all the little things, but the general atmosphere was one of this kind of fear, nerves being shattered, weakness because of lack of food and lack of exercise, and a continuing feeling of helplessness as time went on and on.

How did you receive advance notification of these searches?

Because [Mr. Drente] worked for the SS. Since he worked for the headquarters, which happened to be in our [old] house—they had occupied the house that we lived in as the SS headquarters—since he worked there he would hear or see the bulletin or know that this was going to occur.

Did Mr. Drente ever bring you reading material?

No, no, he never brought anything. He was sort of illiterate, so his daughters would bring. But the underground, when they did come, would come in with thirty, forty books at a time.

How would they bring books?

In the evenings by prior arrangement, by leaving them on the boat that this man had anchored in front of the house and this man then would go out and bring them in. Occasionally they would bring it in themselves. A few times medicine had to be gotten and this man would know who

Herb, Hertha, Edith, and Nathan DeLevie, 1946.

to contact and somebody would bring it. It was never the same person; it was always somebody different who would do this. On two or three occasions I did actually see the person who brought something.

What type of reading material did you get?

You name it. I went through an entire library from children's stories to philosophy, geography, you name it. I must have read over 3,000 books in that period of time, most of them twice. And to this day I can pick up a book I haven't read, but it's an older book and I read it and I know I've read it but I just don't remember where, the particulars of it. Yes, anything that was printed, we read. Didn't make any difference.

Did reading serve as an escape for you?

I would assume so. There is no doubt that—what was there to do? You either sit and do nothing, you either get into an argument about who was using what for that time, toys were being destroyed, you get sick and tired of playing Monopoly. And besides my drawing, which I liked because I was good at it, and the reading, there was nothing else to do. And this was twenty-four hours a day. You can only sleep so much and after a while you can't sleep, you can't move around, there's really no place to stretch out, you can stand in the corner, there's not sufficient chairs to go around, what do you do? You do what you can.

Could you get any exercise at all, even just pacing around?

How do you pace around a small room filled with that many people? When we first were there, yes, we did some morning calisthenics and so on but after a while there's just no way. There's too much stuff laying around, your bunks, even though you roll them up and put them aside during the day, you still—six, seven adults and five kids and a small confined place and there's just no place to move.

Did you have a daily routine with the tutor?

To some degree. We continued to get up when it got [to be] morning because people got up, you woke up, and you had to go to bed when it got dark because you couldn't afford to have a light be seen from the outside. So we had some flashlights and some candles but basically you could not do much at dark. So the daytime hours was the only time to do something. In the morning we had a washbasin, we washed ourselves. The pail of water was brought in usually, and then we had whatever breakfast there was, whether it be a piece of bread or leftover beans or whatever was there, and then we would study or read or whatever. So we had a couple of hours of what was called quiet time. The education, because of the different ages, was very general, and this fellow was fairly good in math and the languages but the other things didn't amount to that much. So what we ended up doing is discussing the books that we read and whatever we got out of the library and this was done for a couple of hours a day. At first it was much more intense. You'd do two, three hours in the morning, two, three hours in the afternoon. But the fellow couldn't take it and us kids couldn't take it and the parents couldn't take it because they had to be quiet while we were doing this. They couldn't go anywhere either, and they got bored with it, and it got on their nerves. So it became much more on a one-to-one basis where you could quietly sit in the corner and do something. So that way everybody got an hour, two hours a day, but not at the same time.

What did you study?

Math was organized. We studied philosophy, discussed philosophy, and that was based on the books that were available. Geography was an open discussion as to what everybody knew about the world. You played games like naming the countries of the world and their capitals, the biggest river, the biggest mountains, and these type of stuff, and we had an atlas and we looked them up—these type of things. The physics and biology were again—outside of the basics, were based on what we could understand from the books that were coming in. Some of the concepts were very far out and some of them were totally erroneous. A formal line of education wasn't there after the first six months, because basically we had exhausted what he knew because of the concentration. I mean it was an ideal learning situation if you had the mental ability, and the mental ability is very surprising, but the power of concentration is very, very difficult. It seems to become less and less even though you have nothing else to occupy your mind. It seemed that your mind is so occupied with your physical discomfort and the negative vibrations, I guess is the modern word for it, that float around you that you're constantly a bundle of nerves. Every sentence you have to read twice and nothing seems to stick, and that was the case in almost all of us.

Were you afraid because there were people constantly in the house?

That's right, and it was a very small house. Everything could be heard, like you could hear everything that happened in the kitchen and you never knew who would be coming in. It was just established. You talked in a whisper. If somebody was there you didn't talk at all.

Did you know if someone was in the kitchen?

You could hear them come in, yes, and like I say, you could hear almost everything. So, yes, we talked in a whisper. When I say whisper, it was a whisper. You could not cry. If you were punished and you cried, your head was stuffed in a pillow. If you were in pain, if you had stomach cramps or any kind of a pain, whether you're an adult or not, sound was something that just could not be made. The rule was adhered to. It was necessary.

Was there a semblance of a family situation? Did the parents still act as parents?

Well, your parents remained your parents. The problem was more [with] the overriding what the other adults would say to the kids that were not theirs. My father and his brother were very close all their lives, but for my uncle to say something to me, that was like waving a red flag in front of the bull. Especially after a while, "How dare you pick on my children! Look at your own," and vice versa. So everybody kind of did their own thing and everybody was afraid to go over a mark of criss-crossing. You had to keep some kind of discipline. My father was fairly well in charge for most of the time because he was the strongest willed, and that of course led to arguments also. But he still was the strongest and he did lay down the rules and kept them enforced and that, too, was necessary because without it we never would have made it either. Everything kind of interlocks. You do what you have to. You face the circumstances and you must live within it or leave it. And if you're leaving, all right. We didn't because we felt the choice was not really there.

Did you maintain any religious practices while in hiding?

Yes, we did. As a matter of fact, we *davened* [prayed] every morning [to have] something to do. Yes, we kept the holidays the best we could, at least observed them by name. The religious practices, the *davening,* morning, evening, doing Shabbas services, filled time, therefore they were done. Religion was discussed quite a bit, again as a time filler. The big problem was that nobody that was with us knew much from anything because all of us, my parents and us kids, were too young to know much, and my parents were also educated by indoctrination. My father could read [Hebrew], not well. He knew what to observe, what was the proper thing to read, but not a word was understood. He had a couple of *tefillot* [prayers] that were translated in German and Dutch but everything was Hebrew to Hebrew so it was just a question of reading and no way to understand what you read and recalling what it was about because of their prior education. It was quite limited. It was more a dogmatic adherence to tradition, which we did.

What happened when you heard about the Normandy invasion?

By the time that we had the news of the Normandy invasion, they were already in Belgium, and then the next news was they were already in Holland, and we figured that at this pace they'll be there within a week. Then they were stopped, but now there was hope. I mean, here was freedom so it was like a resurgence of everything and no matter what happened, we were going to make it.

How did you get that news?

This came at first from the man who was hiding us and then an underground person came in again. As a matter of fact, at one time, when we heard that news we were already packing up ready to go and we thought the Germans were leaving and then it turned out that they were reinforcing and more Germans came in. So we had to go back in, and that lasted another five and a half months. . . .

The actual liberation was that the Canadian tank division had arrived in one part of our town and they were held up—our town was predominantly made of canals and bridges—and the canal where we were in hiding was one of the major canals that went into the Stadskanaal main fare and this had a big bridge on it. The bridge was blown, and when we heard that the Canadians were at this bridge we figured that it would only be a matter of moments. For three days they couldn't cross that bridge and then again the man who was hiding us told us that the Germans were packing up and leaving. That's when we packed up and went to the point where we felt we could make contact with the Canadians, and we were ready. We took the bicycles and left, all these people [on] a couple of bicycles, and we packed what little we had and us kids were going to run out except we couldn't. And we were going to scream and we couldn't. We had to go about two kilometers up the canal and we couldn't make it. We met some people we knew about the last quarter kilometer and they practically carried us to where the Canadians were, but the bridge was gone and we could see the Canadian tanks. So the Canadians had a raft and they came and one by one took us to the other side and that was the actual liberation. It took another four days before the Canadians actually were able to cross this particular stretch of canals and secure our city and the rest of Holland.

Could you communicate with the Canadians? Did you speak any English?

No, no. What is there to communicate? You get a big hug and I remember getting a candy bar. But then you didn't need to communicate. They could see with their faces that it was worth it to them, and what we felt, I can't really describe.

After liberation, the DeLevie family returned to their home, and Nathan DeLevie resumed his cattle business. The family immigrated to the United States in December, 1949, and settled in Madison, Wisconsin, where Herb DeLevie attended high school and enrolled in the University of Wisconsin.

A chance encounter with Frank Lloyd Wright resulted in DeLevie's acceptance at Taliesin in May, 1953. He studied architecture there for two years and then worked as an architect in various locations before returning to Madison shortly after his marriage to Monica Freund-Fasslicht in 1964. The couple had two children before her death in 1975; two years later, DeLevie married Deena Slafer. He died on October 4, 1989.

*   *   *   *   *

Flora Melkman van Brink Hony Bader

Born in Amsterdam on June 20, 1919, Flora Melkman was the oldest of three children in an affluent Dutch Jewish family.

My family . . . would discuss the fact that the Jews were terribly bad off in Poland, in Russia, even in Germany, where anti-Semitism, I was told, was bred and was fed to the Germans with mother's milk. That was what my mother told me: there is a latent and a dormant anti-Semitism and we Dutch Jews were very very fortunate because our population was very beautiful. Jews were very assimilated. We were allowed to have any profession we wanted, our schools were wide open, our universities did not even at times ask what your religion was. Nobody bothered to know if you were Jewish or not Jewish, but you didn't hide

WHi3187/BDR/1/24

Melkman family at the seashore, Holland, ca. 1934:
(l. to r.) Flora, Duifje, Hartog, Rebecca (aunt), and Anneke.

it either. We were proud to be Jews but not to the extent that we had to say, "I'm so proud to be Jewish," because we lived with everybody in peace. Holland is a place where you could disagree in a very agreeable way. Everybody would admire you for your own convictions. We did not have the need to conform, we had the need to be an individual, and that was fed, as a child, that idea—be yourself, and you will be more admired than if you just follow the crowd. And this was how I saw Holland. We were as free as you feel yourself to be [in the United States]. We had freedom there, totally, and also the insight to help other people. [There] were always committees for the German Jews that came to Holland, there were always committees for the East European [refugees]—*Verein* [association]. There were committees to help anybody, and everybody came to Holland.

What did you know about German aggression in other parts of Europe?

Everything. I read the paper fervently, I was aware because of the people who came in great streams to Holland, reading, material things, and then listening to the stories. Thinking that maybe it's a little bit exaggerated. Later, when I took up all the readings, all the materials, I was strongly inclined to believe that this doom would not just pass us by. I had a feeling it would come to Holland, . . . and my mother would say, "Stop reading those books. You read too much."

Did you discuss your feelings with your family?

Oh yes. I would tell my family that it would be wise if we could try to leave Europe, and my mother said, "Stop reading those books." I was without my fiancé. He was in British India, and I wanted to get away and I wanted to marry him but I had promised [to wait] and my mother promised me [that when I was twenty-one I could marry him]. But by the coming of the war she refused to fulfill her promise because I wasn't twenty-one, and her philosophy was, "If he loves you he will come to Holland." We were thinking, reflecting, that Holland would never be involved, for which I do not blame her—now.

What did others around you think?

Others around me were thinking what many people think here, "It cannot be possible, it is exaggerated, and we will never be involved; it's good that we are good to the refugees, but we will stay out. The House of Orange will protect us. Holland was always safe during every war. The last war we were not involved; the 1914–1918 war left Holland neutral." That was the opinion of every Dutch person: we are neutral.

Did you hear about Hitler's threats to the Jews?

Of course. I believed, but that involved the German Jews. It did not involve the Dutch Jews. We are Dutch Jews—they cannot destroy us. And then the fact that we were decades, ages, centuries without anything in the form of persecution in Holland, it was a dream that it was not possible for the Dutch Jews [to be threatened].

How did people react to the refugees' stories?

What many people say now here, "It couldn't be that bad, or they would not have been here. They did survive, and we can only hope and pray it will not be here and we will be safe." It is the belief of a person that every disaster can come to the next but not to yourself personally. You want to believe that what you hope will come. You never accept the very bad things until it is happening to you.

What did you hear about concentration camps and labor camps?

We did not believe it. We did hear the concentration camp stories of the people that came from Europe. We never knew about any camps that were *Vernichtungslagers* [extermination camps]. We heard about camps that they were making for people in order to get cheap labor. I personally believed everything of it, but there were many people who refused to believe the stories, even if [they saw] people who'd escaped with marks, maybe one in a million. [The people who did not believe would say,] "How did he come up? If it was so bad, how did he then survive it?" It was great disbelief to believe the unbelievable. To think that human beings could inflict [such horror] upon others was unbelievable, especially for the Dutch mind, when never, never anything like that was allowed. We professed a freedom like America did. We instilled in people to be good to each other. In school we had great respect for any religion. We had Indonesia as a colony; therefore, many Indonesian people came to Holland to work, to visit, and mostly on vacation, and we were respectful and correct. We just could not believe that any people would violate those laws that were being conducted by our government, by our press, by the Royal House of Orange, where there was so much love and freedom and wisdom that it was, for our minds, impossible.

Tell me about the beginning of the war in Holland.

Do you know the movie *Gone with the Wind?* It had its premiere in one of the most luxurious theaters in Amsterdam. Elsje [Koopman, a friend of mine,] and I received tickets for that. It was a Friday afternoon. . . . And as I went to bed Thursday night, I had all my beautiful clothing out. Everybody that was somebody was at that premiere and in the evening we were offered a big dinner and gorgeous surroundings. It was the most elegant surroundings in Amsterdam.

During the night I woke up and I thought somebody was fooling around with the garbage cans . . . with those metal covers. I heard as if somebody [banged] the cover down, up and down. So I opened my eyes and I thought, "Who would be in the night in the backyard?" and it became more clear to me that it wasn't so. I looked out the window and I saw flames with little black puffs of cotton coming out of them. And when five would be over, ah, but eight would come, and if eight would come, ten would come, and it was so powerful that I started perspiring. And I thought, "What can it be? That can't only be Germans."

So I went to my mother's bedroom. I had such a devotion for my sister that I didn't wake up my sister. I went to my mother's—this is my father and mother's bedroom, but Father I had already cleared out of my life because he [had had a stroke]. Whatever was done in the house was with Mother. So I went to Mother's bedroom, I said, "Mom, we are invaded." She said, "Did you dream?" I said, "No, these are German planes." She said, "My child, I wish you would leave me alone. You are crazy." I said, "Let me put on the radio"—there was no television. She said, "Oh no, I don't wake up the household." I said, "Come to the window." I took her to the window, and she saw the flames. We turned on the radio, and we heard that during the night we were invaded. I started shivering as if I became very ill. My mother looked at me and said, "My child, what is there to worry you? So we have an invasion." I said, "Mother, do you know what it means? Do you know that we will not have peace?" She said, "I have always paid whatever there was to pay. Businesswise I have kept all the things up. I have no debts, we are an honorable family. There is nobody who can do anything to us."

*Israel and Flora van Brink
on their wedding day,
Amsterdam, Holland,
November 27, 1940.*

WHi3187/BDR/1/26

Despite the obvious danger, Flora's fiancé, Israel van Brink, who had been
working in India, returned to occupied Holland to be with her, and on
November 27, 1940, the couple married.

[The wedding] was all in black, because I was well aware that Europe
was in mourning. It was no time to celebrate a wedding yet. As I made
my wedding plans, . . . I said, "Mother, this is only for our household.
I will marry without a great ado." And she told me, "Flory, you are
my oldest, and you will be the only child that I will see into marriage.
I will not see my other children marry. Will you allow me to have a
family dinner in my house with my sisters?" I thought, "My very, very
dumb mother is not aware of how serious our condition is." However,
I didn't find it in my heart to say no because I knew this would be also
a good-bye to the whole family, and I said yes. "But how do you get
meat and how do you get—?" She said, "Leave that up to me." I think
she must have sold part of our home in order to have the dinner that
we had that night of my wedding. [We] had a very simple *huppah*
[wedding canopy], and after that we had a beautiful reception in my

parents' home and after that the family sat down to our last dinner together—my wedding.

Over the next two years, restrictions on Jews mounted. Although the Jewish Council had given the Melkmans and the van Brinks special exemptions from deportations, they were aware that it was only a matter of time before they, too, would fall victim to the Nazis. Flora van Brink's brother, Hartog, was taken for forced labor in January, 1942.

[My parents] had to close down the business. That meant no income. [First] no gentile person was allowed to work for Jews. Then [the law] came [that] no Jews should have people working for them, even other Jews. . . . We lived in the Rijnstraat behind the store and next to the store, so our Jewish customers would come as visitors and leave with poultry. So part of the household was taken up by what was our store. Our store was empty. . . .

My husband and I decided to eat with my mother. I lived in the same block [as my parents]. I gave my household money to my parents and I would eat there and tell them that I don't like to cook alone with my husband and that I'd much rather have the same company that I had. So my mother cooked and we ate every evening with my parents and then leave at a quarter to eight to go to my house, because after eight you were not allowed in the streets. It was a time of great fear, but we did not know what would happen. It was the inconvenience of it all that I thought was temporary. I thought, if this is the only thing that they bother us with, we can overcome.

Until in 1942 we all of a sudden heard that there were camps being made in Poland and Germany and that the intention was not to keep us in Holland. A lot of Jews did not believe it, and I also thought this is just malicious undermining of our capacity to survive the war.

I thought we could survive there, but the *razzias* [terror raids] started. My brother was taken from a library on the corner where we lived and taken to the Johannes Vermeerstraat, where the German *Kommandantur* [headquarters] was, on a Saturday afternoon. In 1942, Broertje [Little Brother] went to the corner and didn't come home. Days, days, days, weeks, and my mother turned gray. And we thought he would be deported. . . . And then my brother came back. . . . They just let him go free.

What was life under the occupation like?

We tried to survive by putting the households together and also by my mother trying to work with a *Sperr* [exemption, from the German for "separated out" or "special"], a thing in her identity papers that [said] she worked for a firm that was exempt from being sent to Germany, which of course now we know it was foolish; then we believed it was sent by heaven. . . . We were inclined to stay away from everything that was called dangerous. Now, sheer walking in the street proved to be dangerous because all of a sudden Holland wasn't Holland anymore. We recognized that the gentile neighbors became enemies. The latent anti-Semitism that did not exist when I was a child, or even when I was in my teens, all of a sudden, human beings, as they are, some belonged to the NSB [Nationaal-Socialistische Beweging (National Socialist Movement), the Dutch Nazi party] and openly were our enemies. . . . So whatever would go on in the street they would point out that the neighbors are doing. So what we decided to do was to go out as little as possible.

We heard . . . what was happening in the Jewish *Viertel* [quarter], where we lived far removed from. There were boys lined up on one Saturday afternoon in front of the Portuguese synagogue where my mother was married. . . . The first *razzia* was there. They halted the boys, made them do exercises in the open, and as they were doing that they were kicked in the face. . . . At the end of the afternoon, some were released and some were sent to Mauthausen, I believe, was the concentration camp.

And as it came to the south part, where we lived in relative peace, Jews among gentiles in the streets. We were stunned, we were horrified. [Something like this had] never happened. And then when the laws came that the Jews couldn't participate in traveling, the Jews couldn't do business. All of a sudden after that there was a decision for the Dutch people. On [February 25, 1941,] we woke up and the city was a ghost. Nobody went to work. A strike. But a strike as eerie as you cannot imagine in your wildest dreams. No bus, no baker—everything was being delivered at home—no milk, no lights, no police, nothing. The dock workers started in Amsterdam. This was gentile people who were totally free to do whatever they want; they were so one with the Jewish population that they felt it could not happen. . . . But of course, that lasted maybe [two or three days]. They took out at eight in the morning, six in the morning, all the male population of that square, placed them in front of the beautiful flower parks that we have in Holland, and killed them in front of their wives and children. After that, the strike broke. Nobody dared to lift a finger for the Jewish population, except a very, very strong underground movement and very prominent Jewish people who went into the movement.

And also, for the first time, the Jewish Council was formed. There was no knowledge of the concentration camps. That came in 1942, when we were told to make a sack ready to take the most necessary belongings and to leave. That was when in our block people would jump out of windows, mainly people that had very pleasantly lived there that came from Germany and that had more knowledge than we had. A lot of people in our block committed suicide. A lot of people tried to save their children and had surgery, had doctors who were willing to operate on their children. I know of one man that was a widower with a beautiful young daughter, and he had the daughter in the hospital for an appendix surgery, and she died in surgery. My own husband, Is, had a doctor who was willing to perform surgery on a football knee in order for him to not meet the deadline. . . . We figured out what we could do about that. Now, little did we know that that would be his doom, because when he came in a concentration camp with a cane, he was doomed to go to the gas. Can you see how crossed we lived and what an eerie world we lived, because initially that surgery saved Is?

And when he came home after the surgery, in the Rijn Street, in my house, we had a bay window, and on a sunny afternoon out of the blue sky, a car from the SS came in our block and started getting the Jews out of the houses. They had the lists from temples that we belonged to and charitable causes that all the Jews supported and according to that list they knew exactly where the Jews were. So they would run into these beautiful new buildings . . . you would see them with the German shepherds—that's why I still cannot look at a German shepherd dog— they would go up and get the families out. Now, in Holland it was very normal that the older people lived with the young. It's not like here. If a mother was widowed, they would live with the children. There were beautiful homes and room enough. It would be that a family was doomed to come out of their houses; the *razzia* was there. So the children were dressed warm, the people were dressed warm, but the old mother was not dressed quickly enough or could not grasp it all and did not come out quick. We would see scenes where the German shepherds were sent up stoops, the big stoops that went into those houses, and they would take out a woman in her sixties, seventies that was not so quick to follow the children. And the woman would just hit her head, [bumping down the stairs], and would be just one piece of meat. That made you so sick and so bewildered that when I watched it—and of course I couldn't, these were neighbors, people I grew up with, friends—I would question the sanity of it, and I would know that it was nuts to work for people who wanted us to work; they wanted to destroy us. And that set my mood for escaping them.

> In January, 1943, assisted by non-Jewish friends, Flora and Israel van Brink went into hiding. Flora's parents, Salomon and Duifje Melkman, and her sister, Anneke (Anne), were captured in a March, 1943, *razzia*. They were taken to an Amsterdam theater, and Flora's mother and sister were offered the chance to escape; Duifje refused to leave her husband, however, and both of them died in Nazi captivity. Anneke, whose health was poor, took the opportunity to escape and joined Israel van Brink's mother in hiding. Flora and Israel van Brink briefly stayed with some acquaintances, the Bergsmas, and then hid in the house of the Bergsmas' cleaning woman. From there they moved to the home of a Dutch detective, Anthonie Gerardus Vingerhoed, whose wife was ill with a brain tumor.

[The cleaning woman's] only motivation was material things. If we were willing to pay her, she would want to take us. . . . She gave us an attic room in a very poor neighborhood. And this attic room was divided in two parts. If you've seen *It Happened One Night,* with the curtain in between the beds, that is how we had. Part of a room. Because in the other bed was another roomer sleeping.

Another Jew?

No, a gentile young man who was living out of town and worked in Amsterdam had rented rooms from her. He, too, was okay, and he knew that we were Jewish and he would get half of what we paid. We paid an enormous amount for that room. . . . We could not come down because she had maybe ten children, eight children.

Who knew that you were there?

Nobody knew—she and the man and her husband. Every Friday I gave her an enormous amount of money. It was disastrous. The bed was full of fleas, the house was filthy. It was absolutely unbelievable to sleep in our fear with another human being with a curtain in between. And I heard my husband moan, "Maybe concentration camp is better," and I said, "How can you say it? We have a corner and a window." Then

I was Anne Frank, and I would say, "Look out of the window and look at the blue [sky]." There was no way, he was totally depressed.

One day, as I was just confined to that room, I heard noise, . . . and before I knew it I faced a man with gray hair, very handsome, and I had a tremendous shock. Next to my attic room was the attic room of the neighbors on the top floor, and that was the neighbor of the top floor who came into his attic room and therefore saw me on the attic. Two doors came out on that attic and I was in front of the two doors. I was airing, I was trying to get some air from that room and I saw him accidentally. He right away felt [that I was Jewish] but [acted] as if he didn't know, and I betrayed myself. He was not Jewish. He introduced himself [as Anthonie Vingerhoed], and I said, "I'm Lainie Veenstra."[1] He told me, "Oh, how nice. Are you . . . ?" I said, "Yes, we are just for a short time here." I didn't say anything and he said, "I bet you would like a nice dinner." And I could not eat [the cleaning woman's] food. We were hungry and didn't have food. I said, "No, thank you very much." He said, "Pride doesn't count. Come on." [My husband and I] entered his home, and I felt a sense of comfort. There were pretty things in the house, it was clean, and there were freesias in a vase. I never forget it. With the little beautiful doily under it and I felt part of being at home but I didn't want to say it. We ate like animals. It was served well, and we went up again. We thanked and I cried. I couldn't stop my tears. . . .

The next day [the man] came up and said—I saw his gun, I saw his belt, he was carrying that. He said, "Listen, I feel that you're very unhappy here. I would like to help you both, but how can I?" "I would like you to come to my home, but I cannot take you away from the other family because it would create envy. Do you have enough financing to continue to pay the amount that you pay now for whole room, board, and everything?" We said yes. He said, "In my house you only have to pay and share what we eat and nothing more." I found heaven; this was heaven. . . . Only the household would know. Nobody else. If there was anybody coming, we had to go up to the attic again. . . .

And now tragedy comes. As I heard that my sister was in the hiding place of my mother-in-law, our detective had to see Jewish people through to Switzerland, and he wanted to make our place free because one Jew could never meet the other Jew in the underground. He asked me if we would want to stay a few days in our room there, that half room that

---

[1] Flora had false papers identifying her as Helene Veenstra.

they had with the neighbors, or if we would prefer to go to my mother-in-law's for a few days. My husband was so dumb and I was so eager to see my sister to tell me about my mother, I appealed to my husband to please go a few days to be with his mother and I would meet my sister. This was in April. But we decided in the evening we would take off our David Stars and we would walk to this house where his mother was. We did that. He rebelled. I said no rebellion, we do it. I took off my David Star and my other identification, he shook, but we both walked. This was April 8, 1943.

We went to this Swammerdamstraat that night. I saw my sister, who told me about my mother and father, how they had left. . . . At around eight o'clock, [we were] gathered in the living room, there was a knock at the door, and three people stepped in. Men from a dream. Creatures that you see in horror movies. [A] Dutch [man] with a mustache telling us, "You are all Jews. You are all arrested." None of us had a star. And I said, "No, we are not," and he said, "Show me your identification." Now I had the right identification because I was in the underground. My sister, who was very nervous, stood up and said to the man, "It's I that you are looking for. Take me. My family has nothing to do with it." Then she gave me away that I was Jewish, of course, but I never blamed her. And he said to Anne, "You come with me, but first sew your David Star on."

My mother-in-law, whose address it was where we were, had in that building made a double closet. Imagine a closet with an extra closet and behind that a hiding place. Before anything could happen or anybody would think of, I saw her disappear and I knew why nobody would see her again. She ran right around the corner and went into the closet and let everybody talk. She was disappeared. Now, I stood up. I said to the man, "Why don't you give us a chance to escape?" . . . He said, "Are you so lazy that you don't want to work for the Third Reich?" I said, "You're Dutch. Don't you know better? We have no chance of working." He said, "Who feeds you that nonsense?" I said, "My feelings, because I see too many things happen." . . .

My husband was talking with this man. Anne was hysterical. She couldn't even sew the [yellow star] on. She was crying, "I did this to you, I did this to you. Why didn't I listen to you? Why didn't I stay in the theater with Mama?" . . . My husband went in the kitchen and he told him—Blonk is his name, a Dutchman—"Listen," my husband said to him, "I can work, but I will be very handicapped if I had my wife there. Why don't you take me? It's more than you bargained for"—they were paid money for Jews—"Let my wife free." And [Blonk] said, "She won't have a chance to escape; where could she escape to?" And my husband said, "She would be able to find her way out of here." He gave the man all the money we had, all the gold, all the jewels we had, and he had also our identification papers. I had nothing. All of a sudden when I was dressing to go out with my sister, I was called to the kitchen, . . . and my husband said, "Flory, I just made a deal. I want you to leave." We had no question that we would leave each other, and [I was] thinking that with my detective we could do a great deal because many people were taken from the Weteringschaus jail by the underground. [The soldier] said, "I want you to leave. This is the deal. You go in the front." And he said, "How old are you?" I said, "Twenty-two." He said, "Much too young. Will you remember me? I'm Blonk, my name is Blonk. Go in front [with] the others. I will give you a sign, and you can disappear." I went to the front room, joined the others, looked for the last time at my sister, and he did so. I don't know how I had strength. I walked through the room, knocked at the wall, and my mother-in-law opened [the false closet]. I went in the closet with my mother-in-law and I heard my husband, my sister, and my cousin—the cousin of my mother-in-law—go down the steps to jail. Because anybody who was found was punished. As if we Jews were not punished enough. But that was their law.

We Dutch Jews did absolutely not believe—even I, who had read *Mein Kampf*—that we would be killed. My greatest fear was that we would have to work and work very hard. That is as bad as I could think it would be. But when I saw sick people go and old people, I was wondering, "Why do they want those people to work? They cannot work." And I was afraid they would be put in barracks and just be wasted and die eventually. But none of us ever thought of *Vernichtungslager* [extermination camps]. So you have to understand that for that reason, so many people resigned [themselves] to the worst. To have it over with was for many Jews better than to live in agony every night and being afraid that [the Nazis] would come in the house and kick them out or hurt somebody, to have it over with was the feeling of the Jews in late 1942.

By the time you hid, did you know already the worst?

No! Oh no, no, no, no—nobody knew it. I heard the worst in 1944 after I escaped. I went back to the detective, Mr. Vingerhoed, who then told me explicitly how he had layers of weapons in his attic . . . and how he expected me to be in a closet with the radio, which was illegal to have, and to listen to the messages being brought in by Radio Orange at ten o'clock every night. For that he had made the same type of closet that I had escaped in. . . .

This saved my life another time when he was invaded by the Groen Polizei [Green Police, the Nazi police force]. That street was raided for Jews and they rushed into their homes. I quickly went into that closet and as I was there I saw the lanterns, the batteries with the flashlights and they were knocking against the exact wall that I was hiding [behind]. . . . [The policeman] asked, "Is this *Judenfrei* [Jew-free]?" And [Vingerhoed] said, "Well, check." And the officers came in and I heard them say, "Juden verstecken sich manchmal. Dauf ich in die Klosett [*sic*] kucken? [Jews sometimes hide. May I look into the closet?]" He had respect because the man was a detective, an officer, and I heard that. I felt so safe I wasn't even excited. I also had come to a point why I didn't care any more. . . . So then they left the house and I was taken out of the closet. Nothing had happened. I was not heroic.

I was not afraid anymore because I was alone. I didn't care. I thought it was crazy for me to have fought so hard for my life. Because in 1944—I had to remember messages [from the radio] like, "Jan carries the bicycle. The bridge and the dog have met each other." Those kinds of messages meant something, were codes. Every night it was in between a report of how well we were doing in London. What was bombarded and what was not bombarded, how successful the war was. Now on that same radio, one night, I heard, "We want the world to know that the concentration camps where the European Jews are being referred to, also our Dutch Jews, are in essence death camps. Roofs are being opened and gas is poured in and people are dying like cattle." And on it went. I was paralyzed. I thought [it must be] propaganda. The blood went down to my feet. I became so sick that I hardly could get out of the closet that evening. And I told the family where I was in hiding that I had heard that. Mr. Vingerhoed told us, "Lainie, don't believe that. That's propaganda." I said, "Do you think that it would be possible?" He said, "No, that cannot be possible. They cannot do that." But of course then it clings in your heart and you wonder, "Is it done? Maybe it's true." That was only in 1944 that first word came.

Of course in 1945, after the liberation, when we confronted people in the Portuguese hospital in Amsterdam who had survived, we knew enough. And the fact for me was at that time when I heard those messages, [I realized] maybe I don't see Israel back with me soon, and certainly not Anne with her sickness, and my father, who had written me in deep despair that life had no meaning without my mother. He was partially paralyzed, had no chance. I was sure that my brother would return and my mother, who was in her forties and very beautiful and very strong-minded and healthy. So I wanted to live for them and be there when they would come to Amsterdam. But as I was talking to the first survivors in that hospital where I went to see them, they were all sick or they all had typhoid or they were undernourished, eighty-ninety pounds. I met a cousin of Israel's who had survived [in the camps] since 1942, one of the first taken in *razzias* [terror raids]. And when he told me the matters, he said, "Don't hope. It's hope against hope." I heard Treblinka and I tried to follow what pattern they had and what date they were taken. I knew they had no chance, that they would go into the gas right away. That is what I had hoped, that they had not survived one day there. They were sent through all in different transports in May 1943. . . .

I stayed [at Vingerhoed's] until 1944, June 6, when much to my dismay, that day Mr. Vingerhoed did not come home to enjoy with me in what I had heard in the early morning hours at eight o'clock. I was in that closet a few times a day, whenever there was a Radio Orange. I was not interested what [the newspapers] printed [because they were controlled by the Germans]; I was in that closet. So at eight o'clock before I did start my duties in the house I was in the closet and then that morning I heard the great day had finally arrived, troops had set foot in Normandy. You have no idea what that meant to me. This was the coming home of my family. I thought, "Oh, he's not home. I will share it with him when he comes home." I could not tell that to [his wife]. It didn't dawn to her what happened there. She was a vegetable. She took medication and drugs. There were no operations available to her. And that afternoon he did not come home. He had tried to help a Jewish family go to a certain place and the Jews were betrayed. As they were betrayed, they turned around and told him, "Thank you," thinking that he was the one who had betrayed him. They caught him with the Jews and sent him to Neuengamme. Of course, we didn't know that day. He didn't come home, period. He was at one *Kommandantur* [headquarters]. That same evening, [his wife] was told [that he had been captured] by her children, who were all working and very uninvolved. They were kind to me, but they thought the father was a fool to do all that work. . . . She turned to me and she said, "I would like you to pack up your things and go." I said, "How can I go? I don't know where to go to." She said, "You Jews betrayed my husband." This was my home, this was my corner where I slept. I think that I then went to a daughter for a little while who was married in the Blassiusstraat.

Members of the Dutch underground arresting a German soldier,
Amsterdam, Holland, May, 1945.

Vingerhoed's daughter?

Yes. And there it was very hard for me. Then I went back and I recall
for a little while in that room but with very great pain for fear that I
would be detected by Mrs. Vingerhoed. It was in that attic room alone
where I heard also the Dolle Dinsdag.[2] Then [Mrs. Vingerhoed] became
totally insane, the woman, totally irrational and the daughters feared
that something very frightening might happen to me. I had to leave.

> Anthonie Vingerhoed had been picked up by the Nazis because of the aid
> and assistance he provided to Jews in hiding. He was sent to the
> Neuengamme prison camp, where he died on April 19, 1945. Flora van
> Brink spent the remainder of the war in the homes of other members of the
> Dutch underground. After the Allies liberated Holland in May, 1945, she
> learned that her husband and her entire immediate family had perished. She
> then joined with her mother-in-law to establish a new life in Amsterdam. In
> the following year she married Josef Hony, who had spent three years at
> Auschwitz and had lost his wife and child. Josef and Flora had a daughter,
> Anneke (Anne), in 1947. The family immigrated to the United States in
> 1954 and settled in Milwaukee, where both Honys obtained work. After
> Josef died in 1967, Flora married Aron Bader, who died in 1979. She still
> lives in the Milwaukee area.

---

[2] Dutch for "Crazy Tuesday," September 5, 1944, when Nazi collaborators in Holland fled toward Germany,
where they believed they would be safe after the Allies retook Holland. The result was the virtual collapse
of organized fascism in the Netherlands.

3

Italy

BY the early twentieth century, Jews had lived in Italy for more than 2,000 years. Prior to World War II, Italy had a Jewish population of only 40,000, less than a tenth of a percent of the country's total. Italy's Jews were fully integrated into most aspects of Italian society, pursuing careers as diplomats, civil servants, and military officers—posts largely closed to them elsewhere in Europe.

For fourteen years after Benito Mussolini and the Fascists seized power on October 30, 1922, Jews generally were not persecuted by the regime. On October 25, 1936, however, Germany and Italy formed the Axis alliance, and Mussolini subsequently encouraged popular anti-Semitism. On November 17, 1938, Italy's first racial laws went into effect, forbidding marriages between Jews and non-Jews and restricting Jewish business and employment opportunities.

On September 4, 1938, the government established a system of forty-three concentration camps to imprison enemy aliens (among them thousands of Jews born in foreign countries) and Italians suspected of disloyalty, a group that included approximately 200 native Jews. Prisoners in these camps were treated relatively well: social and cultural activities took place, children attended schools, and families lived as units. In addition, prisoners worked only to maintain the camp itself. Forced labor did not exist as it did for prisoners in the German camps.

After Italy entered the war on June 10, 1940, the anti-Jewish campaign intensified and the government interned more Jews, but Mussolini resisted Hitler's plan for the deportation and execution of Jews. On September 8, 1943, however, following Italy's surrender to the Allies, German troops occupied the northern and central regions of the country. The remaining prisoners in the Italian concentration camps, most of which were located in the southern part of the country, were set free. But nearly all Italian-born Jews (who had not been imprisoned) lived

59

*Mayer Relles, Rabius,
Switzerland, June, 1944.*

WHi3187/RLS/1/5

in cities in the north, and the Germans began mass deportations of Jews
to concentration camps in eastern Europe, where approximately 8,000
Italian Jews, most of them from Rome, perished.

Throughout the German occupation, Italy had an active and effective
underground, which combined with the Catholic Church to shelter many
Jews within Italy and to help numerous others escape to safety in
Switzerland or in Allied-controlled southern Italy. Because of this
assistance, approximately 80 percent of Italy's Jewish population survived
the war, including Mayer Relles, a Polish-born rabbinical student who
was living in Venice when Italy entered the war.

Mayer Relles

Mayer Relles was born in Skala, Poland, on June 2, 1908, one of nine
children of an impoverished carpenter and his wife. Relles received a
secular education in Lvov and Borsczow from the mid-1920s until 1932.
Because of quotas imposed on Jews in Polish universities, Relles, a
promising Talmudic scholar, went to Rome in November, 1933, to study at

the rabbinical seminary there. In December, 1936, he moved to Venice, where he served as a ritual functionary for the Jewish community while continuing his schooling at the university in nearby Padua. His work and education ended abruptly with his arrest at the time of Italy's entry into the war in June, 1940.

What were your duties in Venice?

My duties were cantoring, teaching, *shochet* [ritual slaughterer], and chaplaincy. . . . Usually the congregation had a rabbi and two people, they call them *capiculto*, which means they [were ritual functionaries]. They were teachers in the school in the ghetto. . . . Both of them [performed] the ritual slaughtering, and both of them were cantors, and both of them were chaplains. We had one hospital, Ospedali Riuniti, a big hospital for I don't know how many, hundreds or thousands of beds, and at that time when I came they even had a room for Jewish sick people and a kosher kitchen there.

Could you describe the Venice ghetto?

Most of the people were not Jewish people in the ghetto, because it was the first ghetto to be constructed—that's what they say—and one of the first Napoleon destroyed when he invaded Italy. Of course, during the Middle Ages it was surrounded by water and by a wall, and it was built high—it expanded in height because they could not expand in space.

They had five synagogues: one synagogue is Spanish, one is German, and one is Levantino, and I don't remember [the others]. I know that one synagogue has the walls covered with twenty-four karat gold. Now they have made a museum out of it. . . . [When I was there,] in the wintertime they would have [services] in the Levantino because it was smaller and was less cold because they did not heat it. In summertime they would have the services in the Spanish temple, and the German temple, *Tempio Tedesco,* they had very few people. . . . We used to have *minyan* [quorum of ten men] morning and evening. Why? Because we paid *minyan* men. We had six or seven *minyan* men paid to come to synagogue, morning and evening. Most of the time they were taken from the rest home, which was in the ghetto, too. . . . Saturday, we had very few people, maybe twenty, thirty people, maybe forty, maybe fifty, not more. . . .

The ghetto is there a square, they call it *Ghetto Nuovo* [New Ghetto], and there on one side you have the synagogues, on one side you have

Ya'akov Lifschitz, Chief Rabbi of the Jewish Brigade, reads from a Torah scroll at the rededication of the Great Synagogue, Venice, Italy, May, 1945.

the rest home, on the right side you cross a bridge, a very small bridge, you go and you have a school. . . . It was made for a hundred pupils at least, but we didn't have that many. When I came, we had about thirty students, four or five classes. The people in the ghetto, as I say, were mostly Christians, because the Jews lived everywhere. When you come from the depot side, *Ponte delle Guglie* [Bridge of Spires], there is a tablet made of marble, written in the eighteenth century, that [says that] Christians and proselytes are not allowed to come to the ghetto.

Jews came to Italy to escape the Nazis, right?

Yes, oh yes. Mussolini said that the Jews would bring him prosperity and they are free to come, and thousands of them came from 1933 [on]. Many of them came and stayed in Rome, most often in Milan. I don't know about other cities, Torino [Turin], Genoa, but I know in Venice [there were] not too many. And Mussolini was very much for the Jewish people, especially in 1933 and in 1934 after Dollfuss was murdered[1]—in other words, when the friendship between him and Hitler cooled off, he was very, very amicable to the Jews. . . . In 1933 or 1934 there was a fair in Bari, and Palestine had a pavilion. [Mussolini] went in there and he says that where were the Germans when these people—the Jews who were in Palestine, they had already a country and a high civilization—[the Germans] were still half-naked, roaming in the woods. He wanted Hitler to know what he thought about it. . . .

Not too many [Jewish refugees came] to stay in Italy. Why? They didn't have the means. All they could take from Austria was just a pittance, a few marks, twenty marks or forty marks, I don't know. Enough to buy bread and a little food to eat. So, most of them would come to stay for a while and go away. Where? There was another place where people could go—Shanghai. And strange enough, it was already occupied by the Japanese, I believe—Manchukuo [Manchuria], Shanghai. There, in Venice, the consulate would give visas to whoever came. Yes, but those people who wanted to go, they did not know the way, they did not know [how] to speak [Italian]. They needed somebody, and this was my job.

After Italy entered the war, Relles was taken to a jail and interned for six months in Campagna and in the Ferramonte concentration camp.

---

[1] Austrian Chancellor Engelbert Dollfuss (1882-1934) was assassinated by Nazis on July 25, 1934.

The jail was something I can never forget. It was the worst thing. It was a place you never get used to it. . . . They kept me isolated, no meeting [with others]. The food I could have, for lunch at noon, they gave you a good soup and a pound of bread. In civil[ian] life, I never had such good bread. But who could eat? Who could eat? I smoked. I smoked six, seven, eight packages a day, sixty, eighty cigarettes a day. And sleeping—I couldn't, because there were so many bedbugs. They attacked me day and night. They were not afraid. They were in the thousands. All they give you there is a place to do your physiological needs. There was a place in the wall like a chair to sit down and there was here like a table, and dirty as dirty can be. Lack of air and hot. . . . I really wanted to die. I was there from June 17 to June 30, and I do not believe I slept two hours. . . .

[One day] at about seven o'clock came a policeman, opened [the door] and said, "Domani, lei va a casa," which means "Tomorrow, you go home." And when I heard this I just fainted. And after I came to myself, I said, "No, it's not true." . . . He said, "Yes, it's true. It's written here." In other words, he did not have me on the list of those people who have to be taken care of, and the next day, I was called to the office. They gave me everything back what they took away from me—money and my watch and this and that—and there was a policeman waiting for me. . . .

We [traveled to] Campagna, a small town in the province of Campagna. I'm telling you, never did I see such a beautiful town, a town with beautiful parks, monuments. It's surrounded by mountains, this is why they selected this place. Outside were boys—all boys, no women. Polish, German, a very few Italian, Jewish boys, very few Polish boys, not Jewish. . . .

There was one military barrack and one carabiniere barrack, Concetto and San Bartolomeo. I was to go to the Concetto and those boys brought me up. I came there and there was a young boy and he brought me a bed, he brought me pillows and sheets and blankets. . . . And there I passed from July 3 or July 4 to August 18. It was the most beautiful time I had in my life. Why? Because the government passed me six and a half liras a day. . . . [For] a liter of oil, I paid a lira. A good lunch cost me three and a half liras. They gave you an appetizer, vegetables, spaghetti, meat, eggs, *dolce* [sweets], and wine. Mail—free. You could write a thousand letters and a million cards.

I did not like to sleep there upstairs, so I wanted to have a private room. So I took a private room. The head of the camp, the commissar, he was such a wonderful man, really like a father to us. . . .

We had carabinieri—policemen—and that's all. And they were just to help us, to help everybody.

Were you treated better than the other prisoners because you were a religious official?

No, no, no. I was just like any other man. . . . When I came to live in my room, that night it was a terrible thing. I had a battlefield. [The bedbugs and lice] attacked me and I killed scores of them. But the next day, I learned something. I learned it from my father. He used to do it when they had a wedding and we had ants. We made cake and the ants would attack the cake. He would put the cake on a big table and put the feet of the table in a glass of water, and so they could not come up. In other words, I isolated my bed. But first, I burned the frame, because those bedbugs and the lice are in the frame. They are not in the mattress. . . . I bought a piece of wire [at the pharmacy]. I put cotton on the wire, wrapped around, and I burned that frame all around, those iron springs. . . .

I remember when we left that this was, if I'm not mistaken, on August 18, on a Saturday night. The buses came to take us to Ferramonte, this was already in Calabria. Not all the people, only from the *concessione* [agency] where I belonged. About 200 or 300 people. Those people in Bartolomeo were still left there. The buses came about seven, eight o'clock Saturday, but we left at one o'clock [a.m.]. . . . When we were there waiting to leave town, every once in a while a lady would come or an old man would come, a jar of strawberry jam or raspberry jam or apples for food. Everyone brought something to us, with blessing.

Were you assigned to work at Campagna?

No, we had no work. We were treated just like a soldier, without duties of a soldier. When I left the *caserma* [barracks], when I left the barracks, I had to go three times a day to the police. . . . So I just had to appear, and that was all. We could buy everything, we could go to the library. There was not one place closed to us. . . . At nine o'clock we had to stay in our rooms and barracks, but very few people observed this. Even after twelve o'clock it was like a beehive in town.

Tell me about Ferramonte.

We left on a Saturday, one o'clock, I believe. All day it was terribly hot
and then when we came into the trains it was terribly cold. All night
the director of the police he came, he said, "Gentlemen, I want you
to know that according to the law you should be manacled. But I
guaranteed for you." . . . We arrived not to Ferramonte but to a station
before, Mongrassano Scalo. We arrived about five o'clock in the afternoon
and [it] was like in a desert—the night cold and the day very hot. And
we zig-zagged with the train. Why? They wanted to avoid bombing. At
that time the English, they would bomb Italy, so they had to avoid it. . . .

From Mongrassano Scalo to Ferramonte we had to walk about seven,
eight kilometers, which means about four miles. When we arrived to
Mongrassano Scalo, we saw not carabinieri but police, and there was
a man on a motorcycle. . . . Later we [found out] that he was the director
of the camp. . . . He looked so grim, he looked kind of sour, and [the]
first thing he said, "Only those who are very tired and only the old people
will ride in wagons." Wagons—two wheels, made of two wheels, with
one mule, a mule, and it could contain five, six people, maybe ten, and
there were very few [of them]. The young people had to walk. Second,
he told us that this is a concentration camp. This is not just a resort
place, as we had in Campagna. This is a concentration camp and we
will have discipline, we will be subjected to law enforcement, fascist.
Otherwise, he said, we don't have barbed wire, fences. He said, "There
is nothing of this. But where do you want to escape? We are in a desert,
you have no place to escape. And if you will observe the laws, you will
be happy and we will be happy."

We began to walk, and when arrived there . . . people were already
in the camps. In Ferramonte, we lived in barracks. Every two barracks
had a court—between the two barracks there was an empty space. In
every barrack there were thirty-five people. So two barracks had seventy
people. On one side there was a kitchen. Close to the kitchen was the
bathroom with showers. The water was yellow and full of minerals, and
it smelled like spoiled eggs. On the other side there was in the barrack
a big dining room. . . . It was a dining room and also a library and
like a living room—it was everything. . . .

Outside, it was terribly hot, [but] inside, [it] was very comfortable.
Between one bed and another there was a certain space. The beds had
mattresses and sheets and blankets and pillows and everything. There
were people who worked in the kitchen, and they were paid by the
government. The *piantone* [orderly] . . . was paid by the government.

. . . Each seventy people, they had their own kitchen. They would have a man who would go to Tarsia, accompanied by a policeman, to buy all this stuff. Everything was rationed, but the poverty of the population in that place in Calabria was so great that even what was allotted to them for the rationing, they could not buy. So practically we could have everything to eat we wanted, without rationing. . . . They understood that prisoners have to have clean water, and that stinky water we used only for washing ourselves, to have a shower, to rinse things. To cook and to drink . . . they built pipes underground so that we had clean water from Tarsia.

How were you treated physically?

Physically, we had a real vacation, because food, we had more than we wanted. We could eat turkey as much as we wanted. I was in the kosher barrack, so we would eat turkey—we had a *shochet*—turkey, chicken, eggs. The Fascists themselves, they would bring us, at least you could buy. People from the village around, they would bring things. They were not allowed to come into the barracks, . . . and we were not allowed to go outside. But they would come and stand at the entrance, and we would wait for them, too, and the sentry—there was always a sentry— he would say nothing. And there was an officer, a lieutenant of the Fascist police, when he saw the arrangement, from one side the peasants or the farmers, with their produce, vegetables and eggs and fish and food, and when he saw the refugees from the other side, he would go away so that as to say, "I don't see anything what you are doing." And we would go out or they would come in and we would get the produce and they would get the money, and that was that.

We had only one who was bad, a Fascist, the doctor, the doctor. We had a doctor who took care of us. Every other day they had to give us shots and he had a needle—we used to call him the [black]smith—and he used to shout, and he was always sour. He would not beat anybody, God forbid, but we used tricks on him, terrible tricks. For example, he had two Jewish helpers, doctors. Before getting the shot one of them had to put a little iodine, so he would put the iodine like he already made the shot, and that's it. This is the way we used to fool him. The Fascists, I remember a sergeant, he would come and cry for us because three times a day he had to make an *appello* [roll call], and according to the law everybody had to stay at nine o'clock in the morning, at noon, before eating, and in the evening, [stand] at attention and so that they could see whether everybody is there. But when he came no one was in

Jewish Historical Museum of Yugoslavia, courtesy U.S. Holocaust Memorial Museum Photo Archives.

Prisoners in barracks at the Ferramonte concentration camp,
Italy, ca. 1940–1943.

the barrack. So he went around, "Please, gentlemen, what are you doing to me? I need you, you understand, you cannot treat me this way." And he would always talk and he would laugh and that was that. One day he talked his soul out, and he says, "You see behind here, behind these hills or mountains, we are getting such a beating. The English, they beat us as much as they want. They beat the soul out of us and we deserve it because we should never have become friends with the Germans. They are our secular enemies." The policemen, the police, they were always in civilian clothes.

Later on, we had people, they were called Bengasini, from Benghazi. Why were they called Bengasini? These were Jews from Galicia, from Romania, Polish Jews. They were going to [Palestine] on a boat and the Italians captured them. But the Italians were afraid that some other— Poles, maybe English or German—might shoot at them and destroy them. . . . They were entire families. . . . I don't remember how many families—maybe a hundred, maybe more. And from Tripoli, [the Italians] brought them to Benghazi, which is in Africa, too, and from Benghazi to Naples. In Naples they put them in jail, and from Naples they brought them to Ferramonte. . . . Of course, these Bengasini, the children, needed instruction, and right away the Jewish people made a school, and I was one of the teachers. And right away, by some miracle, we had things to give them a *merenda* [snack], which meant marmalade, jam, and eggs—children needed it—milk, special for the children. The director of the camp graciously cooperated. He would take a load of children in the truck and take them to Tarsia just to make them see Italy, to make them enjoy a trip.

What nationalities were in the camp?

Jews and Yugoslavs, Yugoslavish Jews. We had very few Polish people, I don't remember how many—non-Jews. Lots of German Jews. Very few non-Jews. When I came, we had three synagogues, not one, and one church.

Three synagogues in the camp?

In the camp, yes. It was made—just a barrack with benches and they put an ark, with a curtain, a *Sefer Torah* [Torah scrolls] we got, I don't remember from where, we had two Orthodox synagogues and one Reform, and we had preachers and we had teachers and we had everything. . . .

[Later on] things were different. The rainy season began there—no snow—and we had leakages through the roofs. And we had lots of mud there because it was not plastered. Food, we had enough. The light was very dim. Why? Because you were not allowed to attract airplanes, enemy airplanes. And it began to be gloomy. . . . As long as we had summer, it was much better. [The rainy season] was a bad period.

Then, all of a sudden, on December 20 . . . a boy comes and says to me, "The secretary told me that you are going home. You are free." I believe I fainted. I don't remember, but it was something I couldn't believe. So I ran to the officer and the man says, "Yes sir, you are going. But I can't understand why they sent you to Venice. Why didn't they send you to Padua? But this is something you will make out. It may be a mistake. I have to send you to Venice." I said, "Am I going with a policeman?" "No, this time you are going free, alone." And so I went. He says, "At eleven o'clock you have a train going to Mongrassano Scalo and from Mongrassano Scalo you go to Cosenza and from Cosenza you have the train to Rome and from Rome you have direct to Padua." He made the ticket out for me. . . .

When I arrived in Mongrassano Scalo, there was a very small station— one man. . . . He said, "The train to Cosenza left just this very moment, and you will have to wait until tomorrow morning." So he said, "After all, you are not in a desert. Sit down and you will be here with me. I am sitting. You will sit here with me." A few minutes later a Fascist militia[man] came—he had to go to the front. All he had with himself was a bread and a can of olive oil. . . . And he took out his bread and he put the oil on the bread and put it in the oven there and fried it, and all night he gave me that bread with olive oil. And in the morning I took the train.

After his release from Ferramonte in December, 1940, Relles returned to his position in the Venice Jewish community and completed his studies in Padua, receiving a Ph.D. in Italian literature and philosophy in 1941.

What do you remember about the German occupation of Italy in September, 1943?

On the radio Badoglio[2] says, "We just concluded the peace with the Allies and now the Germans, we do not want to hurt them, they have all the

---

[2] Marshal Pietro Badoglio (1871–1956) was the Italian leader who succeeded Mussolini after he was deposed on July 25, 1943, and who surrendered to the Allies.

freedom to withdraw and to leave our country." At that time I worked for the shelters. I wanted to work, I wanted to do something. . . . I was sitting in a bomb shelter, and I heard speeches from the English radio and from other radios telling them, "You Italians, you have to take the arms away from the Germans" and so on and so on. This was on a Thursday.

On Friday morning my boss, the man who was over me in the shelter, said, "It's very bad, because the Germans are disarming the Italians." . . . After the Germans came, they did not hurt Jews in Venice or [anywhere] else except in Rome. In Rome they started, I believe, October 14, 15, 16, they deported Jewish people and of course they were seen in Padua, closed wagons, and the Jews in Venice and other cities said, "Well, we must not lose our heads. After all, the Jews, they were too much triumphant when Mussolini fell. They were too much in rejoicing and this must be a punishment. Nothing will happen to us." The Jews were always optimists, especially the Italian Jews. They said, "Oh, here it won't happen like in Poland. After all we are in Italy. After all, my father was a lieutenant and my grandfather was a captain."

After Germany invaded Italy, Relles attempted to escape into neutral Switzerland but was caught near the border and held near Como. The Italian underground rescued him, and he hid at a Catholic home for the chronically ill in Milan, where he remained until his escape into Switzerland in April, 1944. Relles returned to Venice in September, 1945, and married an Italian woman, Ida Banon, the following April. The couple eventually had three children. Relles served as a rabbi in Ancona and Trieste from 1946 to 1951 before immigrating to the United States. For the next twenty years he held teaching and rabbinical posts in the Chicago area and in Superior, Wisconsin. In 1971 he went back to Italy and served as chief rabbi of Trieste for five years before returning to Wisconsin, where he accepted the position of spiritual leader at Anshe Poale Zedek synagogue in Manitowoc. After retiring in October, 1992, Rabbi Relles and his wife moved to Goleta, California, where the rabbi died on August 18, 1995.

4

Lithuania, Poland, and Ukraine

BEFORE World War II, nearly 6.5 million Jews lived in eastern Europe. Although Jews had lived in Poland, Russia, Ukraine, Belorussia, and the Baltic states as early as the tenth century, anti-Semitism was common, as were official discrimination and pogroms.

Poland's 3.3 million Jews constituted 10 percent of the country's population and 30 percent of its urban residents. Jews fared relatively well under Jozef Pilsudski, who had seized power in 1926, but anti-Semitism became rampant after his death in 1935. In 1936, Jewish ritual slaughter was banned, and two years later businesses were forbidden to operate on Sundays. On December 3, 1938, the government announced its sponsorship of legislation to reduce the number of Jews in Poland and to eliminate Jewish social, political, and economic influence.

On August 23, 1939, Germany and the Soviet Union signed the Molotov-von Ribbentrop nonaggression pact, in which each side pledged to refrain from attacking the other. The agreement also contained a secret protocol in which the two countries divided up eastern Europe into spheres of influence. World War II began on September 1 when Germany invaded Poland; the Soviet Union sent its troops into Poland two weeks later. The fighting ended quickly: the Soviets controlled Latvia, Lithuania, Estonia, and eastern Poland (i.e., Belorussia and western Ukraine); Germany annexed northern and western Poland; and the rest of the country came under a German civil administration. Jews in the German-controlled areas were immediately ghettoized and required to wear badges identifying them as Jews. Mass deportations began in December, 1941, and continued throughout the next three and a half years. When the war ended in May, 1945, only 380,000 Polish Jews had survived, more than half of them in the Soviet Union.

In accordance with the nonaggression pact, the Soviet army took control of Lithuania on June 15, 1940, and the country officially became part of the Soviet Union in August of that year. The status of Lithuania's 250,000 Jews (10 percent of the total population) generally improved under the Soviet occupation, although about 7,000 were exiled to Siberia and other areas of Soviet Asia, where many of them died as a result of the harsh conditions. A year later, on June 22, 1941, Germany invaded the Soviet Union and quickly occupied all of Lithuania and Poland. The Jews in those areas fled, joined resistance units or the Soviet army, or went into hiding to avoid falling into Nazi hands. The systematic extermination of Lithuanian Jews began less than two weeks later, on July 3. By the end of 1941 only 40,000 Jews remained in Lithuania, most of them in ghettos located in Vilna, Kovno, Siauliai, and Svencionys. The surviving Jews were subjected to forced labor, and most of them died during the course of the war. In preparation for withdrawing from Lithuania in the summer of 1944, German troops shipped 10,000 Jews to concentration camps in Germany, where many of the Jews died. A total of about 8,000 Lithuanian Jews survived the Nazi occupation. In addition, another 25,000 survived the war in areas under Soviet control. The stories told by Harry Gordon, Lucy Rothstein Baras, Walter Peltz, Henry Golde, and Rosa Goldberg Katz illustrate some of the experiences of Jews living in Lithuania, Poland, and Ukraine.

Harry Gordon

Harry Gordon was born on July 15, 1925, in Kaunas (Kovno), Lithuania, a city of about 150,000 people, 35,000 of them Jews. Gordon was the only child born to Orthodox Jewish parents whose families had lived in Lithuania for many generations.

Tell me about the Russian invasion of Kovno.

It was a complete surprise. And [until] after we seen the red star and sickle, we didn't known that it was Russian tanks. Right away we got scared; we started running back home and tried to hide. We thought maybe that it was German tanks. We didn't realize what was happening.

How did things differ after the Russian takeover?

First of all, they started giving Jews a lot of high positions in government. Like, for instance, let's say in the food situation, delivering food to the Russian Army was Jews. The Lithuanians hated it. Jews started feeling

Harry Gordon (seated, front center), with his parents,
Yakob and Eva (at left), and uncle and aunt, Abraham and
Ettel Gizelter, Kovno, Lithuania, ca. 1928-1929.

a little more respectful, especially the younger generation, around twenty, twenty-five. Jabotinsky,[1] the Zionists—they used to start giving the Lithuanians a lot of trouble. So then the Lithuanians started getting more anti-Semitic, very anti-Semitic. They couldn't express themselves. There was an order out of the Russian government or the Russian military that, first of all, no Lithuanian could call a Jew—call him a Jew. He could get six months in jail. No prejudices, there couldn't be any prejudices. If there was a job opening, whoever come in, and if he's qualified for a job, he had to get it. [They couldn't discriminate] because he's a Jew or he's a Lithuanian or whatever he is.

What happened when Germany and Russia went to war in 1941?

The German ambassador didn't deliver the declaration of war until 7:30 in the morning. The war broke out at 4:30 [a.m.]. At 4:30 the airfield, the airfield in Aleksotas, Russian airfield, was completely demolished. The Russian army didn't know whether it was coming or going. At 12:00 [noon] the Russian soldiers [were] running from the front lines. One was running without boots, one was running without a gun. They were asking for food. There was no leadership. That was a complete mishmash. So then we decided that we know that the Germans are coming in, that the Russians won't stop them, so we tried to go with the Russians, run with the Russian army, run about 250 miles. We wanted to go to the Russian borders instead of falling into the hands of the Germans. We known what was going to happen. But we only got about 250 miles, 300 miles.

How did you travel?

Just walking, sometimes in wagons, some trucks—Russian soldiers, and we asked them, "Do you want to take us for a ride?" Will they take us with them? When they say yes, we went and jumped on the Russian trucks. We were seeing Russian soldiers riding on horses and all of a sudden from a house there comes out a machine gun—the Lithuanians. And they machine-gunned a whole platoon of Russians, maybe twenty-five, thirty Russians. Horses and men, dead bodies all over the place. . . .

---

[1] Vladimir (Ze'ev) Jabotinsky (1880-1940) was a Ukrainian-born Zionist leader who in 1937 proposed a ten-year plan to evacuate 1.5 million Jews from eastern Europe to Palestine.

We heard all kinds of noises, 4:30 in the morning, Sunday morning, all of a sudden—what is happening? I run out of my bed. I got scared, so I run up to my dad and I said, "Hey, did you hear that?" The whole house was shaking. "What's that?" "Ah," he says, "the Russian planes are making maneuvers. Don't worry, go back to bed." Ten minutes later the same thing happened, the whole house shivers. I jumped out of bed again then ran to the windows, then all of a sudden, the airfield, we could see the airfield right from our house, full of smoke. That's all you seen is a bunch of smoke. He says, "I think it's trouble."

So we went outside and then all of a sudden we hear the radio, the news. We put on the radios. Everybody started hearing the news that the Germans had attacked the Russians on the Lithuanian front, or wherever it started there, and the airfield was already in flames. There wasn't a plane left. Then the [Russian] pilot [who was living in our house] came back. He says, "Nobody from my military—nobody's there. No planes. Everything is in flames," he says. "I got to run." I said, "Where are you running?" He says he's running back to Russia if he can get there.

Where did you and your family run?

Yanovo.

Why did you stop there?

We heard that the Germans . . . dropped paratroopers. We were only 250 miles [from home, but] the Germans were already 500 miles on the Russian territory. So what's the use going down there? We're never going to reach it, so we might as well turn around and go back. . . .

My mother wasn't with us. She was in a Jewish hospital. She was sick already before the war started. She had at that time appendicitis. . . . The operation was okay, everything was okay, but then she got an infection and it got worse, because now appendicitis is nothing, but [at that time it was more serious]. As we came back I wanted to go and find out, maybe I can take my mother back home, maybe she's better already, because she didn't know we left and we didn't know what was happening with her. And when I went to the Jewish hospital I had to push myself through fences. I know on the roads how to get through there but it was quite a ways to get there. And can you imagine the Germans? I was walking by Germans with Lithuanians and I was walking right straight by them and I thought maybe they're going to stop me or they're going to say, "Hey, Jew boy." That's all I needed.

Courtesy Yad Vashem.

Lithuanians beating Jews as German soldiers look on,
Kovno, Lithuania, ca. June 24, 1941.

But anyway I made it to the hospital, and it was a complete Jewish hospital. There was 500 patients. I got in the hospital and when I got up to where the secretary was sitting, or whatever, by the window, and I knock on the window, and I said, "My name is Harry Gordon. I want to see my mother. My mother is here." . . . She closes the window and says, "Wait a minute." And I know it wasn't the same girl who was sitting there when I brought my mother in, when we took my mother in. She was Lithuanian, she wasn't Jewish. So right there I was a little suspicious of the whole works. She opens the window and she said, "I'm sorry. Your mother is dead." "Can I see my mother? Can I see her? Where's the dead body? I want to see her dead body." She says, "Why don't you go down in the basement because [that's] where they keep the dead bodies."

I went down to dead bodies. There was a doctor there, a Lithuanian doctor. There wasn't a Jewish doctor. And I said to him, "I want to see my mother." He says, "There's 500 patients here." I said, "Five hundred? What do you mean 500 patients?" He says, "All 500 Jewish patients. They're all poisoned. They all poisoned them. How are you going to find [your mother]? When they are poisoned they all look alike. How are you going to find your mother's body?" When I heard that, I just ran out of there and I went back home.

Following the Gordons' return to Kovno, they were herded into a ghetto
with the rest of the city's Jewish population; Harry's father was deported
shortly thereafter. For the next three years Harry was shuffled between the
Kovno ghetto and forced labor camps in Lithuania. Then, in the summer,
1944, he was shipped by cattle car to Dachau, where he dug ditches for the
disposal of corpses. In April, 1945, troops from the U.S. Seventh Army
were approaching Dachau.

At that time, then, the Americans were already in Germany, and they
were close to Landsberg am Lech'. Dachau wasn't too far from Landsberg
am Lech' and the last order of Hitler was to finish off all the rest of
the inmates of the concentration camp, to take them to the German Alps
and to finish them off, not to leave any witnesses. So they put us in
boxcars, open boxcars. There was no closed boxcars, but open ones.
They put us maybe 200 to 250 in a boxcar, and then they started taking
us to the German Alps.

But the Americans were that close already. They only took us about
fifty to seventy-five miles, between Munich and Landsberg am Lech'.
And for the first time, all of a sudden, [we saw] English planes. [The
train] stopped. And then English planes came down and they started
machine-gunning the front. They killed about 500 to 600 people and
they knocked the engine out of commission. The idea was that they
thought that was German soldiers escaping from the front lines. A half
an hour later, I don't know if it was the same planes or other English
planes, came down and then all of a sudden we all started waving our
Sing-Sing clothing, our jackets, our pants, or whatever, our caps, whatever
you were wearing. They were so low that I think they could see it. They
realized it wasn't German soldiers, that it was prisoners, and they didn't
bombard it, they didn't machine-gun anymore. But that engine was
knocked out of commission, and the Americans were already only about
fifty to seventy-five miles away.

Two and a half hours later, another engine from Munich, another steam
engine, came, hooked up again, and started pulling us farther. But they
pulled us only for another ten or fifteen miles and then they stopped.
It was by a little woods down there, and the German guards were watching
us with machine guns or with rifles. They jumped down in the woods
and they didn't let any one of us [escape]. They said if anyone tries to
escape, if anybody tries to jump, they'll be shot right there. But we
understood, we could see, that they were pretty nervous. . . . Some of
them had their civilian uniforms in their packs. A lot of them guards
already run away but the real Hitler fanatics . . . were still laying in
the woods and waiting so that nobody would escape.

That night it started raining. It was around 12:30, 1:00. Me and my uncle were in the same boxcar. We jumped from the car and we started walking in the field. . . . I remember I had a heck of a time pulling my legs out of the mud. But my uncle was in better shape than I was, somehow. And it was pouring, it was raining. I'll never forget it. It was terrible. So all of a sudden we seen a big barn. We didn't know where we are, but we known this must be a farm barn or something. So we said we got to get out of the rain, anyway, and see what's happening.

So we got in the barn and there was a lot of hay laying so we hide ourselves under the stacks of hay and we lay there until the next morning. . . . All of a sudden we heard all kinds of voices, couldn't understand, we thought maybe soldiers or somebody's still looking for the escapees and German soldiers. But then all of a sudden we hear Polish, French, and then they started, the Polish guys, started lifting the hay with their forklifts. They were feeding animals, so they needed the hay down there and all of a sudden they took up the hay and all of a sudden they seen two guys laying down there. So they said to me and my uncle in Polish, oh yes, he heard last night that there was a big trainload with Jewish prisoners coming through, and a few of them, they said, escaped. So he said this is not a too safe place. He says he'll put us over in a different place. He put us in another corner, and they covered us up with hay, and they said a little while later they're going to bring us food.

An hour later they brought us some milk, warm milk, just right from the cow. Can you imagine warm milk and bread? I haven't seen that in five years. And I started eating and drinking that milk and then all of a sudden . . . it was coming from the top and going to the bottom and, oh, was I sick. Then the Poles, every hour they used to come in and say the Americans are only fifty miles, thirty miles. I think it was on a Thursday or Friday when we escaped, and by Sunday morning they came in and said the Americans are six miles from here. I said, six miles, we could walk to town.

I didn't have the pep or the power to walk; I don't know how I kept going. My uncle was in pretty good shape, but I had a hell of a time. When I got in town I seen American MPs with Red Cross wagons, with ambulances running from one place. And I kept hollering, "I need a doctor, I need a doctor." I remember Americans, they put me in an ambulance, they opened up the ambulance and some Americans were taking pictures. They put me on the end gate of a truck, of an ambulance, and they started giving me chocolate with cigarettes, and they were taking pictures and I keep hollering, "I want a doctor. I'm sicker than a dog." So we ran into a Jewish guy, I don't know who he was, but he says,

"There is a basement. There is for all the sick ones who can't move," he said. "They lay right there by the basement." So I went. You had to walk about a block or two blocks until I seen people laying down there so I lay down with them. My uncle says to me, "I'll be back a little later." He says, "I'm going to look around, maybe I can see somebody from our family or friend. Maybe I'll find somebody from our *mishpocha* [family], and I'll see you later." It was in the morning around 9:00 or 9:30. In the meantime somebody came up, some American, and he started telling us that we'll have to stay here until they can make room in the hospitals. The hospitals are filled up with German prisoners. They've got to evacuate it to make room for us. . . .

Around 4:00–4:30 in the evening ambulances started driving up and they started taking us to the hospital and it was in Wiedergeltingen by Landsberg am Lech', and then as they put me on that stretcher and they took me to the first time even for a shower and that wasn't for a shower like they call it in the gas chamber—that was a real shower. I'll never forget it. Two American MPs were standing with guns. Two high Germans—they were colonels or whatever, in German uniforms—and [the Americans] were watching them. I was laying all undressed, a skeleton, that's all I was. First of all, they wake me up, they put me on the scale, but I couldn't move. And it weighed exactly fifty pounds and I didn't believe it. And then they took me and they started scrubbing me and washing me, and for the first time in five years I had a shower. After the shower was done, then they put me in a hospital bed.

After spending two years in a hospital, Gordon was taken to a camp for displaced persons at Bad Wörishofen, where he met and married a Polish survivor, Genya (Jean) Lelonick. In March, 1949, the Gordons immigrated to the United States and settled on a mink farm belonging to Harry's uncle at Bear Lake, Pennsylvania. After several months, the couple moved to New York City, where Gordon found work as a garment cutter. Dissatisfied with life in New York, the Gordons moved to Madison, Wisconsin, in 1951 and had three children before divorcing in 1969. Harry Gordon held a number of jobs before becoming a self-employed scrap metal dealer; he retired in 1992. Gordon has published an account of his Holocaust experiences, *The Shadow of Death: The Holocaust in Lithuania* (Lexington, Kentucky, 1992), and he continues to speak about the Holocaust at schools.

* * * * *

Lucy Rothstein Baras

Lucy Rothstein was born on August 15, 1913, in Skalat, a half-Polish, half-Ukrainian town that was part of Poland until 1939 but is now in Ukraine. Her family consisted of her father, Wolf, an orthodox Jewish leather merchant; her mother, Gusta; and two younger brothers, Joe (b. 1919) and Milo (b. 1923). After graduating from high school in nearby Ternopol, she attended law school in Lvov. In 1933 a law banning Jews from the legal profession forced her to abandon her schooling, and she learned the tailoring trade, returning to Skalat to open her own shop.

If you went north of that marketplace [in Skalat], that was the nice street, the nice neighborhood, and they called it the Corso. When evening came, you know what young boys and girls did for entertainment? They put on their better clothes after supper and they went for a walk. And they walked on that Corso from one end to another, sometimes ten and twenty times during the evening. If you were a little courageous, you walked out a little farther to the north, where there was no more sidewalks, and these couples who went a little bit more, they were already suspicious. People talked about them because they left the sidewalk and went out to the north. Of course, it was that kind of city where people didn't have much to do and developed lots of talk. Gossip was a great part of entertainment. If somebody saw a girl with a boy once, they said, "Oh, they probably date." And if they went off the sidewalk to the north, they probably have kissed already. And so on and so on. You can imagine. That was the kind of life that people lived in those days, and that was entertainment.

Did you attend synagogue on a regular basis?

Not the kids, but my father went every Friday evening, every Saturday evening. If he could, he would go on a weekday, but most of the time he prayed at home because he didn't have time to spend time on the weekday, had to go to the store. Women didn't go to services much. My mother went only on High Holidays.

Did you keep the traditions in the home?

Kosher, yes. Everything was kosher—two separate dishes, and [we] celebrated every holiday and every semiholiday like Chanukah and my mother cooked and baked the traditional dishes for the holidays. . . . In fact, in those days there were very few people who did not keep kosher. Among the 3,000 Jews that lived in Skalat, I doubt ever there were more than ten families who didn't keep kosher, and there were very few who would use a carriage on Saturday, who would drive on Saturday. There were very few cars. No Jew had a car before the war. There were some gentiles who had cars but very few also.

WHi(X3)39320

Rothstein family, Skalat, Poland, 1925: (l. to r.) Wolf, Joe,
Rifke Feige (grandmother), Lucy, Milo, and Gusta.

Were any members of your family nonreligious?

No. They were all religious—in fact, very religious. . . . The younger
generation did not wear beards but they all kept kosher homes and had
kosher meats. It was a very, very rare Jew in Poland—not only in Skalat,
in Poland—who did not buy kosher meat.

You attended a Hebrew school?

I started Hebrew school when I was five years old. I started it before
I started public school. But the Jewish community was so poor they could
not keep a teacher all the time. So whenever they brought a teacher he
would stay like one year and he'd leave because they didn't have money
to pay him. A year later they brought another teacher, or two years later.
So I had started at Hebrew school many times. Every time there was
a teacher my parents never failed to send me. But I had to start from
the beginning because every teacher who changed started a new class.
. . . Once I started high school, I couldn't go to Hebrew school because
I didn't have the time. When I was in high school, I had to teach other

children from my same classroom so I get paid because tuition was very high and my father couldn't afford to pay all that. So I couldn't go to Hebrew school.

Were most of your friends Jewish?

Yes, yes, definitely. The groups were very divided and in grade school, if we sometimes had non-Jewish friends, we had to bribe them so that they don't tell the boys to hit us. The girls and boys had separate schools in grade school, but it was in the same building. As I told you, Poland was poor and they didn't build schools. So it was a grade school probably a hundred years old. The first floor was for boys and upstairs was for girls. And if some girls didn't like some [other girls] they would tell the boys, "Beat up this girl." So very often we had to bribe the gentile girls, and we were not close with them.

> In September, 1939, the Russians occupied Skalat and the condition of Jews
> in the city improved. Rothstein acquired a position as a credit officer in a
> bank. But circumstances changed rapidly after June 22, 1941, when
> Germany declared war on Russia and moved troops eastward. In July, 1941,
> Nazi forces overran Skalat and murdered about 400 men, including
> Rothstein's father.

[The Germans] came in the middle of the night, Friday to Saturday. In the morning my father got up, and he put on his Sabbath clothes—he wants to go to synagogue. In order to go to synagogue, he has to cross through the marketplace, and we had a gentile friend—he was a customer of ours, he used to buy a lot in the store. He was a shoemaker, and he used to buy a lot of leather. And he was a very nice man, real premium. And early in the morning he knocked on the door and said to my father, "Don't dare to go anywhere." My father and my brother, Milo—Joe was at that time in the Russian army—they were going to go to services. And he told us the story. He said the Germans came in the middle of the night and this morning they killed already a few Jews in the city, among them a boy who was eighteen years old, had just graduated from high school, from the Hebrew high school in Lvov, and was the only son of a widowed mother, a very good-looking young boy. So he said, "Stay home and hide, because they are running from house to house and taking Jews to work." So my father and brother took off their Sabbath clothes and we put them in the basement. That basement had a trap door from the hall, and we closed the door. What else could we do? Mother and I were upstairs, were in the house.

And then the German soldiers started to come in with young Ukrainian boys, because the Germans didn't know where the Jews lived. Don't forget that they don't speak same language, the Germans and the Ukrainians. The Ukrainian knew only the word *Jude* [Jew], so they showed them with a finger where a *Jude* lived, and of course they broke into our house and there were no men. They didn't ask questions, they just opened the basement and hauled out the two men. And the shoemaker came and told us that they take men to work, so my father and brother put on strong clothes, and we also heard about concentration camps, so we thought maybe they take them into concentration camps, so they put on good, strong clothes. My brother, I remember, wore riding pants and good, new riding boots and a new shirt and a suit coat. And my father was dressed about like that, too. And my father didn't wear riding boots, but good clothes. And that was in the morning, Saturday morning.

In the afternoon they were not back, and we talked to all the neighbors. They had taken all the men from them and nobody was home, so women started to run around the marketplace and look for the men. And of course there were already all kinds of rumors that many Jews were killed and some are working hard. Oh, about four o'clock in the afternoon my brother came back in his pants and barefoot. So what happened? Where is father? "I don't know," he said. "Right away they separated us." My brother worked washing cars and trucks, so the Germans took off all his clothes, left him only his pants. They said a Jew didn't need such good clothes, and then one German told him he may go home, sent him home. But he said not everybody was sent home. That was Saturday. My father didn't come back.

Sunday morning, we heard that there were bodies in the basement of one of the towers [of an old castle on the outskirts of the city]. And one young boy came out and told the story. They put in a few hundred men—statistics later showed it was 400—they pushed all these men inside and threw a few hand grenades. And that boy was not [dead]. He came out in the morning. Nothing hit him. He just lay about among those dead bodies the whole night—he was afraid to move. In the morning when day broke, he saw it was quiet, so he crawled out, of course all bloody, but he wasn't even injured, and he told how it happened. . . . At that time my father didn't come back, but they started to bring every day, the Germans would catch a group of Jewish men to dig graves and bury those, and at the end of the day they shot these. That was going on for a few weeks until finally they formed a *Judenrat* [Jewish Council, the Nazi-appointed governing body of the Jewish community, responsible for enforcing Nazi orders, including rations, labor, and deportations].

Lucy Rothstein, Ternopol, Poland, 1932.

WHi3187/BAR/1/5

German persecution of Jews increased, and a ghetto was established in Skalat. Nazi troops would periodically sweep through the ghetto and forcibly removed people. Fearing for their lives, many people, including the Rothsteins, constructed hiding places in their houses. The Rothsteins constructed a bunker under a false outhouse attached to their residence. Upon hearing that the Nazis were rounding up Jews in Skalat, the Rothsteins and a neighbor boy named David entered the bunker.

Milo was the last one [in] and he put the board on top of the hole from the bottom, put the pail back on, and closed that side board, and we sat there for two days and two nights. Mother had prepared water and bread and a candle and matches there. They were always in there. And we heard upstairs, they had broken into the house and they broke dishes and there was jingling and clattering and everything else and then we heard screaming. Where our basement was, on the other side of the wall was the basement of David's family, and they were taken out and we heard them scream. Imagine what was going on. And of course [we] covered the boy's mouth so he doesn't scream because he heard all that.

That started in the morning. So the first day and night and other day. The second night it was quiet. Early in the morning the same man who recommended us who should build the bunker came. It was also prearranged. He knew where the bunker is, in which part of the kitchen. It was under the kitchen. He started to stand with his feet on the floor and started to yell, "Mrs. Rothstein, you may come out. It's over." And we came out. And then we found out that 2,000 Jews were taken out on that day.

A labor camp was established in Skalat in early 1943. Lucy Rothstein was appointed personal seamstress to the local Nazi overseer; her husband-to-be, Edward Baras, was the overseer's farm administrator. Several months later, Lucy, her mother, and her brother, Milo, fled the camp and hid in a nearby forest because of rumors that the camp was to be liquidated.

Milo and I and mother started to walk toward the forest; where should we go? The forest was very, very close to the village and was also great danger because it was close. First we stopped in the house of the forester. There was a tiny house, a very small house where a very poor forester lived and was right next to the quarry where the Jews worked. And he was known that he used to help the Jews. Was a very nice, very poor man but a very good man, and he would help the people who worked on the quarry. I don't know how he helped them, but somehow he did. He had a good name. We peeked into his window and saw a candle and his wife was feeding the baby, but we figured she would not let us in because every Jew would go to him. There are so many working on the quarry he knew all of them. How could he hide all the Jews?

So we opened the door to the barn and there was a cow. And it was at least warm. It was summer, but it was a very cold night. So we huddled down next to the cow, and we spent the rest of the night there. In the morning the forester came in and he was very scared. He said, "I cannot keep you here." He said, "I have already Jews in my attic. I can't [keep you, and it's too dangerous] here in the open barn." So he took us to the forest and showed us a cave that we should get in there. We still had a little money that Milo hadn't lost. The money was in a different place than the jewelry, and it was not very much anyway, so we gave him whatever we had, to the last penny. We stayed three weeks, and he would bring us a bottle of water and a half loaf of bread, about once a week, sometimes once in five days, so after we had stayed there a few days, I said, "You know what? I'll go and see where Eddie is. Maybe he can help us." I didn't know that he was not on the estate anymore.

I wore that farmer dress still—I didn't have anything else, so I wore that outfit, and I said, "You know, in the evening, I will go." And we were not supposed to be outside when it was dark because there were militia—Ukrainian militia—and the Ukrainians were very bad toward Jews, most often much worse than the Poles. The undergovernment belonged to them—the Poles didn't have anything to say.

So I cross a little bridge and I see an old man with a cane walking, and I give him the Christian greeting. They say Jesus is great, or something like that—I can't translate it exactly from the Ukrainian language. And he answered me in his own language, so I figured somehow, with my glasses, he is not suspicious at all. But he was old, with a cane, he thought that I am one of the village. And I went to Eddie's house, and the front hall—to the right was his door, and straight ahead the gardener lived. And there is a padlock hanging on this door. So I thought, "What should I do?" If I go into the gardener, it's like I mentioned before. He can right away go to the village and bring the police. But we are so terribly hungry that I figured I have to do it. I went in. They talked very nicely to me. They said, "Baras is gone. He had to go in hiding. . . . [The Germans] put a price on his head, and we don't know where he is." I didn't say I'm hungry, but he gave me bread. I didn't tell him that we are hungry, I told him that Mother and I are in a cave. I didn't tell him where. I said we are in the forest, but he knew that every Jew is hungry, so he gave me a half a loaf of bread.

And I go back with that half a loaf of bread under my arm, and here I see the militia, and they are right in front of me, and they recognize me [as a Jew] right away. . . . [They said,] "Let's take her to the office." And I started to bargain with them. I kept on saying, "Please tell me, what will come out for you, what will you gain from that." And you know that I persuaded them. We bargained like that maybe ten minutes, and one of them said, "Let her go."

So I came back to the forest, I couldn't find my cave. I remembered I bent in a little tiny tree that I know where the entrance is—I couldn't find, absolutely. I had to wait until daylight. And of course, my mother and Milo worried inside that I will not come back. . . . Most people when they left did not come back. More not than yes. In the morning my mother crawls out. It was still dark but then I knew where it was. So we had food for another day or two.

After about two weeks in the forest, Lucy's mother returned to town to dispose of some of the Rothsteins' goods so that they could buy food. She never returned. Later the forester told Lucy and Milo that their mother had been captured by the Nazis.

Then that forester said to us [that] he simply cannot feed us. He was a very poor man, I knew that. So he said, "I'll show you where Jews live in the forest." He took us one night and drove us directly to the Jewish group. Many people knew where the Jews lived, but probably very few were willing to show it. . . . [That forester] took us to another forest, quite far from the city, which was much better. And there was another forester, who knew about us. Without the help of outsiders and gentile people, nobody in the forest would have survived. You had to eat—that was the main problem. So he brought us to the group, with which we stayed to the end. Of course, we had to change places very often; there was danger in the forest, too.

How many people were there then in that group in the woods?

A different number of people all the time. When I came to that group, there were maybe ten people. And we also kept on changing our way of living. Like with that first group you would sleep daytime and live nighttime because these people thought that at night when you cook they don't see the smoke in the village. Then we moved to another group, there was just the opposite. They said, yes, you can see smoke, so we changed to normal life. Most of the time I would say the groups were about seventeen, twenty people, twenty-five were some groups. There were a few groups, not many, a few groups in each forest. There were groups there were only six, seven people. Were all sizes. There was danger.

Like summertime we just lived among the trees. At one time we had built from brush, from wood, like a little tent, but you couldn't do it often because we didn't want to break the trees. The more trees you broke, the more bushes you broke, the more footsteps you left, the more danger it was. . . . When you went out you wanted to carry as much as possible so you don't have to go often, because every footstep was a danger. Like one group was once discovered because they carried straw from somewhere. I don't know if it was stolen or maybe some farmer gave it to them. They wanted to sleep on straw. So the straw gave them away. They left marks somewhere. You had to be very careful how you lived.

What kind of daily routine did you have?

Eating was the whole routine. See, when there was a group of twenty, twenty-two, you had to cook. We were a lucky group. We were comparatively the richest group in the forest because there was one family with us who supplied the food. They were quite wealthy and they had connections in the city. They would buy a whole sack of potatoes, these small salad potatoes, . . . and the farmer would bring it to the forest. Of course, every one of us would go once in a blue moon—even I went, my brother and I went, to the city where we had stuff hidden away from the farmers, at the gentile houses. I once tried to go to [a family friend] also, never found the place. I didn't go alone, I went with another man who said he knew the place, but we never found it.

So there were many people who knew that you were hiding but did not turn you in?

Yes. There were four gentile farmers on the edge of the city, four brothers had four cottages. The rich ones never let us in, never sold us anything, not never gave, never sold us anything. But the poorest one of them would always supply, and if one of us didn't have enough money or goods to pay, he said to forget about it. But none of them gave us away. That was besides the forester.

Why did you take that risk?

We had to take the chance. There was no doubt about it. We had to take the chance, yes. When we went to the city, we took a terrible chance, because many of them were killed going to the city. But what else can you do—starve yourself? There was one in another group, but in the same forest, who was afraid to go out for food. He only ate what somebody gave him. People had pity on him and gave him something. Finally, everybody was starving. People didn't want to share with somebody who wouldn't go. So finally he decided he will go. The minute he went out of the forest he was killed. One German and one local man, a gentile, were going hunting. They had the guns with them, and they saw him and they killed him. So it's luck. He never went out; that was the first time he went out. So everybody who went out searching for food risked his life. But still, we considered instead of starving it's still better to die a different death than starving is the worst death. The slowest and the worst.

Were you able to get any additional clothing to help you get through the winter?

Clothing, yes. I went to another farmer, another man, another shoemaker who used to be our customer and also used to help us and I knew that my father's clothes was there. Lots of my father's clothes was there. So Milo and I went to him and he gave us some. So the rest of the war I wore my father's pants and my father's shirts and so did Milo. We went to him and he gave us some clothes.

Did everyone in the group have adequate clothing?

Oh yes, everybody had something in the city, and if [what you were wearing] wore out completely, you'd go and get it. But we all were in rags. For instance, I went to a few places where I had, and once I picked up my good black coat, woolen coat, and it was not the smooth material, it was wool. It had a knotty material, and we walked off into the branches. When we walked in the woods we didn't go on the main road. Of course, we tried through the thickest to go. We hid always only in young forest because the older forest have big trees and it's far from one to the other, like a foot or two. So we looked for those young forests that hadn't been thinned out yet. And you tore your clothes terribly. Especially with that coat that the material was not smooth. I had all kinds of colors of patches on that coat. I had green patches and blue patches and everybody looked like that, and you wore coats, so around the waistline you wanted to have something tight. So you had a rope if you found one, or a string or whatever. If you had a loose coat, you froze. So we really looked something, believe me. And the feet, rags of course. Nobody had shoes anymore. You had your old shoes with open soles and you wrapped them around with rags and rags on top of rags. That's what you all had. Nobody had a decent pair of shoes.

Did you have any kind of religious life in the woods?

Yes. Somehow they always knew when the holiday was and they even had a prayer book with them. I don't know how they got it, but there was a prayer book, and when the holiday came, [they prayed]. I don't think Saturdays, not. Saturdays there was nothing. But we were there during the High Holidays, and they prayed, yes. That was only time as far as I remember, holidays. There was Rosh Hashanah, Yom Kippur, and Sukkot.

Did you discuss how God could be allowing this to happen?

No, this is funny. Let me see, I cannot remember. You know what the main discussion was? If I had a tub of milk I would put myself inside, something like that. And white rolls and milk or a cup of milk and a cup of chocolate and cake and something like that. But discussions about God, no, there were none. Not in our group until after the war. During the war nobody mentioned God. The prayers were mechanical. But after the war there was an awful lot of discussion. Suddenly he came to life, and the people that I knew after the war kept on asking, "Where is God?" That's all. Very few would say God punished us for that or God punished us for this. They only asked where is God. Is he somewhere or isn't he at all? That was constant. But during that time it seems like unimportant. In fact it seems like nonexisting. Besides those mechanical reading of the prayers on High Holidays, I don't recall anything else. It just seems like it doesn't exist. People only talked about food, that's all, about shelter.

Did you talk about liberation or your possible future?

That was constant. The funny thing is, I wouldn't say everybody hoped. There were always two points of view. There were some who kept on saying, "We'll never survive, nobody will survive. Germans will kill everyone to the last one." And there was always from the opposite tent who would say, "That's impossible. Somebody must survive and tell it to the world." So there were completely opposite.

I'll never forget when I went the first time out on a trip to the city and I wouldn't even say I was scared, not at all. Because I figured there's no difference. Most of the time Milo went, he never let me go. He went with other boys. But there were quite a few girls in the group and others went, too, so finally I persuaded him, and I went with him once, only the two of us. That was my first trip, and I remember it was very tiresome, of course, and with those torn shoes to walk and your feet are cold, wet, and when I saw finally, on the horizon, the black outline of the wood, I'll never forget that feeling—"Oh, I'll be home soon, and I'll be able to rest." All we thought about was food, shelter, rest, get rid of the lice, get rid of the vermin, get rid of the rags. That was all. Nobody had serious discussions. About [the] future, of course, everybody hoped, but not many believed. In fact, I myself did not believe that I'll survive. I think it was more luck. Some people say the strong ones survive. Like the saying—Nietzsche says only the strong survive. That's not true. It's not always true; it's a matter of luck also.

WHi3187/BAR/1/6

Edward, Victor, and Lucy Baras with their landlady
and her son, Bamberg, Germany, ca. 1948-1949.

Lucy and Milo Rothstein hid in the woods until the winter of 1943, when
they were liberated by the Russians. Milo joined the Russian army and was
killed in March, 1945. Lucy returned to Skalat and married Eddie Baras on
April 7, 1944. The couple had a son, Victor, the following January. The
Baras family left Skalat in late 1945 and made their way to a displaced
persons camp in Bamberg, Germany, where they remained until May, 1949.

What did the camp look like?

It was barracks also. German soldiers used to live there. So like a family
didn't have a room. You always had to have somebody, another family
or at least a single person. We always had a single man, a stranger, in
the room. There were not enough rooms. But we didn't stay there long
because people who had a child had priority to find an apartment in
the city. We never found an apartment—a room. So in fact when Joe
came back we didn't live in the camp anymore. We had a room with
a private family.

How long did you stay in the camp?

[Until the] summer of 1946. Eddie was longer there because he was on
the police force of the camp. They had their own DP police, so he

went to work every other day—twenty-four hours work and forty-eight hours off. It was like institutional life. You went down to the breakfast in the dining room and then down for dinner. Frankly, I don't remember. He probably would remember better. When we came in they would give out clothes. There was a warehouse, and I think we had mostly dry food, because I think once a day we had only cooked meal. In other words, they would give us packages, those Red Cross packages, where there was cheese and chocolate sometimes and crackers. Oh, now I remember, I'm mistaken, because I remember that we got once a huge can of tomato sauce, like restaurant size.

I had a stove in my room where I could cook one pot. . . . I remember that the baby would get every day breakfast, like in the dining room, we cooked cereal and whole milk. I can't recall exactly how it was, but I know that I was able to make something in the room, too. See, the food was so funny. A family would get such a huge can of tomato sauce. What would you do? It was not organized. You would get more chocolate than the useful stuff. But I don't remember if it was only a supplement to the meals. I can't recall that.

What about religious life in the camp?

Oh, they had services. Not many. . . . I think the Hungarians had the very religious group. But at that time, as I told you, Jews weren't religious anymore, at least not Polish Jews. . . . Most people can't get over it, after all those losses that they suffered during the war. So I don't know which God is better. I wouldn't say there is no God. But if there is, there's only one, so how can he—I keep on thinking, if that one prays on Friday and this one on Saturday and that one Sunday, this one prays standing and this one prays kneeling and this one prays doubled up in half like they're Muslims, what's the difference? You pray always to the same God. And I think most survivors think like I do. You can believe only in one God, you cannot believe in many.

After leaving Germany, the Baras family spent nine months in New York before moving to Sheboygan, Wisconsin, to join Eddie's brother and sister, who had been sent there directly from Germany. The couple's daughter, Ellen, was born in 1954. Eddie Baras worked as a machinist at the Kohler Company in Kohler, Wisconsin, from 1953 until 1974; Lucy Baras worked part-time as a seamstress until her retirement in 1987. Her son's death from leukemia in 1977 devastated her, but she has remained active in writers' groups and has written her memoirs and several articles on anti-Semitism. Eddie Baras died on February 28, 1995.

Walter Peltz

Born in Warsaw, Poland, on May 12, 1919, Walter Wolf Peltz (born Velvel Peltz) was the oldest of five children. The son of a poor woodcarver, Peltz left school at age ten to learn the tailoring trade. The Peltz family lived in the area of Warsaw that would become the ghetto erected after the Nazis occupied the city in the fall of 1939.

Would you describe your apartment in Warsaw?

The apartment [building] that we lived in, there was 478 families. Can you imagine? It was like a city by itself—one building. But I don't want you to be under the impression that each family had five-six rooms. No. The majority [had] only one single room or two rooms, a room and a half, they called it. . . . The front [of the building], there where the ritzy-pitzy people used to live, they used to have three or four rooms. But other than that, there was only one-room apartments.

How many people lived with you?

Five children, two [parents], and my grandmother and one aunt.

Courtesy Yad Vashem.

Part of the Warsaw ghetto wall and the street on the Aryan side.

How many beds were there?

There were only two beds. There were only two regular beds, and there were four people to a bed. . . . The kitchen was in the corner of the room. . . . The kitchen was built out of bricks and stone, that's it. And they had some tiles around, if there was a fancy kitchen, they had tiles around. It had an oven for baking and the only thing you used for fuel is wood and coal. Of course, some people had more money and they lived in more rooms, they had beautiful kitchens, nice kitchens with big stoves. The stove did work on wood and coal and gas, the combination.

How did you heat the apartment?

This was a big problem, the biggest problem really. In the wintertime it was just horrible. You couldn't leave a glass of water on the table, because it did freeze during the night. [For the] children, that was the horrible thing in the morning, to get up. You couldn't stick out your foot because it was so cold in the room. So [my mother] used to get up an hour earlier, or half an hour earlier, to start a fire. We had [a pot] made out of steel and [it] used to get red hot and keep a little warm, and that's how we got dressed. And that thing didn't burn all day long. You couldn't afford to burn it all day long. . . . Now, I'm talking about a city like Warsaw, which it was a big city. You can imagine like the way people lived in smaller towns. Ah, it was horrible—worse yet, worse yet.

Was your family religious?

My grandfather used to [be] the cantor, he used to be there leading the services. He was very religious. My father and the family, they were very versed in Hebrew, and they were very religious. But something did happen. . . . In 1932 or 1933 it was, around the area, they did forbid the Jewish ritual of meat.

The slaughtering?

Correct, kosher slaughtering. . . . We could not, as a family, afford to eat meat every day. If we ate meat, that little that we ate, my mother used to buy for the weekend, for Friday. She couldn't afford to buy a chicken. The poor woman used to buy all the insides and the feet and

the wings and what have you, because it was cheap. And maybe once
a week she used to buy a piece of meat for my father because he worked
so hard. So when [slaughtering was forbidden], kosher meat [more than
doubled in price]. So my father—I'll never forget this—my father said
to my mother, "I don't know what's going to be now. How in the world
can we afford to buy meat, or anything?" He says, "Before we couldn't
afford [it]." And my mother—I'll never forget—cried. She says, "Well,
that piece of beef that I used to make for you before, I can't do it now."
So my father snapped out of it and says to my mother, "Well, if there's
a God," he says, "he knows that we cannot afford to buy that black-
market meat." So he says to my mother, "You go ahead and buy
nonkosher meat and make it kosher yourself."

How did you deal with anti-Semitism and attacks by Poles on Jews?

I was always involved. I always was a leader and always had a group
and we all used to go attack them. And I mean attack. I want you to
know that I was stabbed, knifed, four times.

At what age?

At a very young age, I want you to know. I never did walk the streets
without a weapon in my pocket. I always had a weapon in my pocket,
though it was forbidden. But who did care? I wouldn't be able to live
with myself if I walked the street and I seen a group or a hoodlum or
whoever it is, attacks a Jew that I should take off and run away or hide.
No, that never happened. I always got involved, I want you to know.
That's not only me but a lot of us.

What did your parents say about getting mixed up in fights?

My father always used to tell me, "Hit them first—always. Never duck,
and never run away." He was the same way. I remember when I was
little, he used to do the same thing. He used to stand up for his rights,
used to fight. He never told me not to get hit and run away—never.

After the Germans invaded Poland in September, 1939, Peltz fled Warsaw
for the Russian border but returned shortly thereafter in search of his
family. He discovered Warsaw in chaos, his home destroyed, and his family
starving.

Then when I started to look for my parents, I went back to the neighborhood that we lived [in], and that big building was bombed and it was burned. It was nothing—a pile of bricks, that's all. After a few days I found out where [my family] are staying or living. They lived in a hole in the ground which was supposed to have been an air shelter. I crawled in there, and there my mother was laying on the ground with some straw under her and a candle was glowing. Then I came in and I came closer; she looked at me and she says to me, "Why in the hell did you come back for?" I says to her, "You don't even know where I came from. You don't even know where I was." I says, "Here I came back." I says, "I risked my life. I came back from so far [because] I want to try to help you and the rest of the family." So she says to me, "You cannot help us anymore. This is it." She was laying, hungry, swollen, cold.

And then as I talked to her my little younger sister walked in. The only things that she had on—it was so cold outside—was from a bag, one of those potato bags, those woven bags, a hole cut out for the little thin hands and no shoes. [She] didn't even see me, ignored me, running over to my mother. She was so happy that there were rotten potato peelings in the garbage. So my mother says to me, "See this here? So you better take off. Maybe you'll be the one to save yourself."

I wanted to see the rest of the family, which I did. I talked to them, and the next day the Gestapo was after me [because I'd been involved in resistance activities]. . . . Somebody pointed a finger at me, probably. I've seen death is closing up on me—hungry, no money. I didn't have anything to eat. . . . You know for how long I didn't take off my clothes and I didn't wash myself? I had lice that they were eating me up alive. So I talked to my father and my sister that time. I had to make the decision and to go.

Did you see your family again after that?

No.

Did you ever hear anything about them?

No. So, early in the morning I said good-bye to them and I left and I was walking. It was so cold. . . . I was hungry, and I walked about fifteen or twenty [minutes] or a half an hour . . . [when] looked and I seen my little sister is following me. So I stopped and I called her, I says to her, "Machla, where are you going? Why are you following

Children in the Warsaw ghetto.

Courtesy Yad Vashem.

me?" She starts to cry terribly. She says to me, "Please, take me with you. I want to live, too." I says, "Honey, I don't know if I'm going to be alive. I don't know where I'm going, and I certainly can't take you. I just can't." She got so hysterical that she threw herself on the sidewalk and she started to pound her head on that cement. She was bleeding terribly, and I had to leave her there and went away. That was the last time I saw her. And so then my journey started.

What happened after you left Warsaw?

I came into a town with the name of Miechow [in the region of] Wrablesky. . . . I went into some Jewish people there, and I was hungry. I begged them for food. They were afraid even to help me. So somebody advised me to go to some kind of a Jewish man, a butcher. They gave me his name that he is in charge of the Jews around there. So I went to him and I begged him, I says, "Please, I haven't eaten. I have been beaten." I didn't have any shoes on. I gave away my shoes for a piece of bread. I didn't have any shoes—barefoot. I says, "Please help me." I told him I run away and so on and so forth. I couldn't go through the whole story. So he gave me a piece of paper, he says to me, go to so and so, here and there. He says, "They'll help you." So I says to him—and I seen on the stove was cooking—I says, "Please, why do you send me away? Give me some warm water and a piece of bread." He says, "No, go over there."

So I went over there where he sent me. They wouldn't give me anything. They told me that they [had already eaten] supper. They haven't got anything. So I went back to [the butcher]. And as I was ready to knock on the door again, somebody gets ahold of my hand. And so that guy starts to knock at the door and somebody looks out through a curtain, I seen into the window, and he comes fast to the door, opens up the door, he greets this man like he would have been God knows who. . . . This guy says to [the butcher], "Let in that guy." So he lets me in. So he says to his wife, in Yiddish, "Give him a piece of bread and let him go."

And then when they go into another room, this guy gets up and calls me in. I found out after a while he was a German. He says to me, "Who are you?" So I told him. I started to cry. I just couldn't take it anymore. I started to cry horribly, terribly. So that guy says to [the butcher], "You know, I've been observing this boy," he says, "for the last two hours, walking around the streets." I couldn't walk anymore. I had blisters on my feet; I was sick. I wouldn't care if somebody would have done away with me at that time. "I observed that this boy is going around the streets from this house and that house," he says. "What's going on?" So I start to cry, and I told him, "I'm so hungry. I haven't eaten for days, and I got beaten up." You could tell that I was beaten up. "And I came here to ask for some help, some bread, and they send me from one place to another." . . .

The German says to this guy, "Take a look here." He says, "How long do you thing that that guy is going to last? How long do you think he's got to live?" So he puts his hand around my neck, I must have looked awful at that time, and he says to him, "Take a look. You mean to tell me you send him away. Couldn't you afford to give him something warm to eat?" . . . He says to [the butcher's] wife, "Come on, give him some food." [The butcher] says, "Wait a minute, don't give him anything." [The German] says to me, "Come with me." You know, that guy took me to his house and gave me food. Would you believe it?

After I got through eating there, this man gave me on a piece of paper an address and he told me I should go to these people, and they were Jewish people, and that they'll give me shelter for a night or so. So I did go to those people. When I presented them with that piece of paper and that name of this man, they were very helpful, for one reason, probably fear. This man knew the Jews around very well in this town because he lived there. But when the Germans came in, they did occupy that town, he became an official there. Therefore, his word was taken by everybody, I suppose. . . .

The next day, it was early in the morning, I did get up and I did thank those people for letting me stay overnight, and then I took off to the next little town. The journey to this next town was very horrible to me because I did meet with a lot of Nazis, right there on the highway. They were making headquarters in the woods and they had some tables out and maps, and I had to go through them. There wasn't any other way, and I was afraid if I'll go through they'll recognize me and this is going to be it. So I did hang around for quite a while in the area until I seen two children walking with two loaves of bread under their arm and one canister of milk. So while I was sitting there, so they stopped to start to talk to me and this little boy asked me if I'm hungry. I says, "Well, Son, yes, I am hungry." So he gave me the loaf of bread—he offered me the loaf of bread that I should tear off a piece, which I didn't want to do. But I asked him where do they go. They told me they're going home to the next town. That's the town that I wanted to go to, because I was told that there's some Jewish people there. . . .

So I told them, "I'll tell you what. I'm going there, too. Do you mind if I'll help you carry that container with the milk?" And they gave it to me. They were walking next to me and I was carrying the container of milk and did go through all those Nazis and they thought that I'm probably part of them, so they didn't even pay attention to me. About a half a mile later I gave them back that milk and I thanked them very much and I took off.

I came into this town assured there was still Jewish people there, and I did go into some people and talk to them. As a matter of fact, this one family, a very well-to-do family, let me stay overnight in a barn. . . . I wanted to get ahold of some kind of a family that would accept me that I could stay with them. So a few days later I came into this particular house and I asked for work. So this lady started to ask me some questions, who I was, from where I am, and she recognized that I am a Jew. So, she told me, "Well, I tell you, I would like to help you very much, but if I can trust you—and I hope I can—I've got a Jewish boy," she says, "which I'm trying to hide here, and two I wouldn't be able to do it." So she says to me, "Wait a minute. I think that I can send you someplace. They are very well-to-do people." . . .

[A few days later,] I did go to them. I came to that place and I did go in through a gate, where I was met by two Doberman pinschers.

And as they took off toward me, the lady—I started to holler—called them back and finally she walked up to me, she asked me what she can do for me. So I told her that Mrs. so and so sent me [so] that I might find some work. So, she says to me, "Why don't you follow me?" So I did and we came in the rear of the house. It was a beautiful, beautiful, big house. It looked like the White House, with pillars—just beautiful. It was unusual to see a house like that in an area where such poverty was. . . .

And the way I looked was just horrible, horrible. My clothes were shabby and torn, it was just terrible, and they recognized me right away that I'm a Jew. There's no question about it. So I asked her, I begged her to let me stay. I'm willing to do any work that they'll ask me to do. I don't want any money, only a roof over my head and some food. So they did take me in, and they took beautiful care of me, like I would have been their own son. . . .

There was an incident that over 400 Nazis and Polish police came around there because they claimed that there's a lot of people hiding out in the woods. There were some large woods. And . . . there were Jewish people still living there on a farm and they had visitors from the United States, two girls, and when the Nazis came around there they took them out and killed them. Took them out on a little hill and machine gunned the whole family, which I was told the next day.

When we heard the shooting early in the morning we didn't know what was going on, but we've seen from far away people running from one end to another. So the lady that I worked for, her son-in-law came home for the weekend, and he was a judge in another town not too far away from there. So he says to me, "Son, we don't know what's going on. You better take off and hide someplace. But," he says, "I'll tell you what. Why don't you go out on the field and after a while we'll send out the cows so on the field you are free. Whatever might happen, you got time to run away." . . .

I walked out to the place where they were supposed to send me out the cows and the cows were there already. While the cows were out there—you know, they're animals, they always like to go in places that they shouldn't. [A man named] Kusik bought [coal] from the people that I worked [for]. They used to cut up soft coal from the ground and I used to be in charge of it. . . . When they cut out that soft coal and it looked like large bricks, so you had to put them on the top of each other with air in between so the wind dries them out. So while I wasn't there the cows did go between them and they tipped over some of them. So when I came out there, the first thing, they start to curse me and call me a Jew. "Take a look what your cows did," so on and so forth, and all of a sudden his blood started to boil and he says that he's going to go tell the Nazis that I'm a Jew.

I begged him not to do [that] and he started to go toward the road. It was about a half a mile away from the road. I got in a rage and I beat him so up that he died. Well, I suppose it was me or him, one of the two. He didn't die right away. I hit him a few times so hard and it was right on a point where there were two holes. There were fish ponds there and he fell into a fish pond and I did get ahold of a big rock and I let that rock go on him, too. And while I did it I actually didn't know what I'm doing, but it was too late. I says to myself, "My gosh, what did I do?" So I jumped in the pond and I did drag him out and he was still alive, and he was crying and telling me that I killed him. So I says to him, "How could I kill you that you're still alive? But if you're not going to shut up, I will." So I told him, "How come you wanted to go to the Nazis and tell them that I'm a Jew, that they should kill me for nothing. I begged you not to do." I says, "If [the cows] ruined a bushel of that soft coal, I would have given you ten, fifteen bushels." That didn't mean a thing to me.

At noontime [I] had to take the cows back, so Kusik's wife was afraid that he should come back. He had only one cow, which I did allow him to keep him on that field that belonged to the people that I worked for. And I seen [Mrs. Kusik] from far away coming, it was already noontime, and all of my cows, the thirty-six cows, did lay down on the pasture. So I says to him, "Waclaw, if you're going to tell your wife that I did it to you, I want you to know one thing, I'll finish you and your wife." I says, "I haven't got anything to lose." He says, "What should I say?" So I told him that we heard the shooting and we both—I was wet and he was wet—that we both jumped in the pond and you fell and hit your head on a rock. Because his head got so swollen, it was bleeding. I couldn't stop his bleeding.

My heart was beating like I just can't tell you. When she came closer, she saw [him]. She started to cry and scream and she asked me what had happened. So he told her that he jumped in the pond with me and he got hurt. So finally she told him, "Don't come home because the Germans are running around. They're arresting people." So she went home and brought some bandages back, white pieces of cloth, and some remedies, and she put [them] around his head.

But in the meantime I was afraid to keep the cows, all the cows delaying that they probably might hint that something is wrong, you know. So I took a lot of courage and I took my whip, and I start to give a signal to the cows and they start to take off and I went behind them. As I let them in the barn, I came into the kitchen. The kitchen was huge in that particular place, and the whole kitchen was filled with Nazis and Polish police waiting to be served lunch. This was a terrible ordeal for me to go through, but I didn't know what to do with myself. So finally I went into the barn. . . . Around 3:30 in the afternoon, or 3:00, something like that, they took off.

So when they took off I came into the house and I told them about the ordeal that I had with [Kusik]. He was hated by everybody. This man was a thief, he was no good. I know he was a poor guy, but he was no good. The first thing that the son-in-law asked me, "Is he alive?" I says, "Yes." He says, "It's no good. He's got to be finished. Otherwise you're going to have a problem and we're going to have a problem." So we had to finish him. I was involved and the judge, and somebody else was involved, a third party was involved, was somebody who served the government. . . .

[Mrs. Kusik] came up to me on the street one day, she says to me, "They killed my husband and I'm going to go to the police, tell them that [they're] holding a Jew. You better escape. I'm warning you." She didn't have anything against me. So I says to her, "Well, you're not going to do anything to them wrong. You're going to do it to me. I'm going to lose everything what I've got. They are rich. They know people in the government. They'll buy themselves out. Nothing is going to happen to them, but only to me. Please, don't do it." She says to me, "Nobody's going to stop me."

Toward the weekend, it was in the afternoon, I don't know what time it was—I never knew what time it was, didn't have a watch or anything. The only time the people could tell time is looking at the sky. The chief of the police came from the city, which I did know him, he knew me, too, and I was right there to try to take out a pail of water from the well. So when he came in through the gate and toward the house, I said hello to him and he said hello to me. But the way he said hello to me I kind of didn't like it. I didn't take two minutes. The girl that worked inside came out, she says to me that the Mrs. wants to see me. So when I walked in, the chief was holding some papers, and she had tears in her eyes, she was crying, and her daughter was there. But of course the son-in-law wasn't there, the judge. He was in this town. He only came home once in two weeks. She was crying, and he says to me, "Is it true that you are a Jew?" I said yes. He says to me that Mrs. Kusik came in and did sign an affidavit that I'm a Jew and they are holding a Jew. I says, "Well, she did told me that she's going to do it, but I didn't believe her. She claims that it's our fault that her husband got killed." He says, "Yes, that's what she says." So he says to me, "What can I do?" I says, "I don't know." I says, "At least give me a chance to run away." He says to me, "For my sake you don't have to run away, but if she goes to somebody higher than me I can't do nothing." So he took the papers and tore them up and threw them in the garbage, and a few minutes later he left.

You didn't deny that you were a Jew?

I couldn't deny, I just couldn't. It would have been worse for me. If I would deny that I am a Jew, then I had to prove it or go to court or go to the German government there. I would have to prove that I am not a Jew, and I couldn't prove it. I didn't have any papers. . . .

A few days later I was out with a team of horses. [Mrs. Kusik] came up to me and she says to me, "I want you to know that now I'm going to the Gestapo. I can see that the chief of the police didn't do anything. They probably bribed him." I says, "Please don't do it." So I thought maybe I would scare her. She says to me, "You can kill me, you can scare me, you can do anything to me. I am left with a little girl and they killed my husband and I don't care what's happening to me." So she made up her mind that she wants to harm them, not me. But in the meantime she did more harm to me. In order for her to go to the Gestapo, she had to go about forty-four kilometers to a place by the name of Kamionka.

A time went by, if it was two weeks or eight days or ten days or fifteen days, I don't know exactly, I was sitting eating lunch and a neighbor farmer was there waiting for me. He wanted me to come over to his house to cut up a pants for a son of his. The lady came into the kitchen and her face was terribly worried. She says to me, "Son, I just looked out to the window on the street that I've seen there's so many Nazis and Polish police and I don't know what it is." So I says to her, "Well, it's not the first time." And as she walked out from the kitchen to the dining room, a farmer's son by the name of Jankowski ran into the kitchen and he says to me, "Please," he says, "run away." He says, "There's a bunch of Nazis outside, and the police, they're asking about you."

So I did run to the window, I wanted to get out of the window, there were two Nazis with machine guns right in front of the window. I ran to the door and looked out the door: the whole house was surrounded with Nazis with machine guns. And I've seen this is the end. But at the last moment—it happened so fast—from the kitchen there was a

door, it was like a storeroom . . . maybe twelve by twenty [feet]. It was
going so fast and I started to think what to do. They had a big, huge
box there that they used to keep certain things. So I opened up the box,
I wanted to jump into the box, but the last minute I says, well, maybe
it's no good. So I jumped over the box and I squeezed myself in between
the box and the wall and as I did I heard in the hallway, those heavy
boots and running in and breaking everything.

[It was] a bunch of Nazis and they got ahold of that guy, Mr.
Sczybiersky, that was waiting for me to come over to his house and cut
up a pants for his son. And the first thing, "Where's the Jew? Where's
the Jew?" That's the first thing. And he says, "I don't know, I don't raise
no Jew here." And then the lady came in and she spoke fluent German.
Then they started to beat her and I heard—I didn't see, but I heard—
everything that's going on.

When they came to farmers, the Nazis used to come with big long
heavy wires with a point that they used to go and poke in hay or in the
barns and so on and so forth. When I squeezed myself through that box
and there was a door behind me, they came and poked. . . . When they
opened up the box they covered up that [space] between the wall [and
the box] that I was squeezed in and the next to me was a stepladder
and on the top of the stepladder, a short stepladder, were piled up nice
and straight those potato bags. . . . [The farmer] was not a youngster
by that time. He must have been in his sixties. They took him outside
and made him undress in the nude, put him towards the wall, they had
two guys with guns in front of him and the Nazi told him, if he's not
going to tell where I am they are going to kill him. And he didn't tell.
They didn't kill him; they took him with them. Well, it was going on
for hours and hours and hours.

Finally, when they were writing their report, the lady of the house
was crying horrible and this one Nazi—probably he was the leader of
the whole group—made a remark: "Well, your son-in-law, he's a judge,
and you've been hiding a Jew here. You know what's going to happen
to him." But she says, "But I didn't know that he was a Jew. He was
such a nice boy." And they start to beat her because she tried to defend
me. "So where did he escape if he is not here?" So she said, "Maybe
he found out that you are here, so he ran over to the [river] and from
the river he ran into the woods." They did buy this story.

Now when they left, it was toward evening already, but I couldn't move.
I was dead. I felt like I'm paralyzed from fear. Do you believe that they
closed the door and with a flashlight they looked, they try to look over
where I am, the Nazis, and I felt everything is dying in me. Do you

know what saved me? He leaned toward that stepladder with those bags and all the bags piled up on me. When they left I couldn't get out. When the lady came in and she cried, she says, "Please, Son, why don't you come out?" When I pushed away that stepladder and I seen her face, the way she looked, bleeding, her eyes swollen, you know that I thought maybe I would have been better if they would have caught me.

But when I crawled out from there, she was crying over me. "Where are you going to go? You heard that they mentioned that they'll see me around. They'll come and kill all of us. You know that they mean business now. I don't know what's going to happen to my son-in-law." She says to me, "Where are you going to go now?" I says, "I don't know." She says to me, "Why don't you hang around until my son-in-law will come for the weekend?" She still tried to help me. And they did help me. I want you to know. They jeopardized their lives.

The son-in-law came and I was hiding and I was sleeping a whole week long with a family by the name of Royek. This man took out his children from the bed and put them on the floor and gave me the bed. That's unbelievable. This has only happened one out of millions. This old man that I told you before they had undressed and tried to shoot him because he didn't tell them where I was, they released him during the night and I got ahold of him on the road, and when I saw somebody coming I didn't know it was him. When he come closer I could tell because it was a nice night. So I started to call out, "Mr. Sczybiersky, it's you." He says, "Yes." So he says to me, "Oh Jesus." He says, "Thank God that you are alive, they didn't caught you." He says, "They just released me," and he walked from the city back in the dark. . . .

He says to me, "Son, unfortunately that happened. There's two ways that you can save yourself. Either go to Russia, try to get to through the border," he says. "That's that, anyway," he says, "What have you got to lose? Or to get ahold of a passport and go to Germany as a alien, as a worker." So I says to him, "Well, as an alien to go to Germany, I haven't got a chance. I'm going to try probably to go to the Russian border." He says to me, "I would like to draw you a map and the directions where to go, but I'm afraid. If I draw you a map," he says, "if they'll catch you they'll torture you, and you'll have to tell them that I did it or somebody else did it." So he says to me, "I'll tell you what I'm going to try to do. The only thing is if you want to draw a map yourself, I'll draw it on the paper, [and then] I'll destroy it after a while." But I did, I drew a map on my pelvis.

After successfully hiding for more than a year, Peltz surrendered to the
Nazis. He was then sent to the Majdanek concentration camp in Poland.

I gave myself up because I couldn't take it anymore. I was bitten by dogs.
I was sick. I had blood poison[ing]. I couldn't go to a doctor. I was
filthy and dirty. I didn't take off my clothes for weeks or months. I had
so many bugs in me that I just couldn't take it anymore. I was thinking
of committing suicide but I couldn't do it. . . .

[At Majdanek] I worked for about two or two and a half or three
months, give or take. [I] worked very close to the crematoriums where
they used to gas people. It was very, very simple. For example, they
had that gas chamber, the gas chambers that they had, isn't the gas
chamber that you've seen pictures of, like in Auschwitz and so on and
so forth. The gas chamber was almost what they did portray in *Holocaust*,
in the [television] movie. They built a building, if you want to call
it a building. It was made out of concrete and it was the size, I would
say, a little larger than a two-car garage, and it had two doors—a double
door in the front and a double door in the rear and they had signs, like
people should think they going to take a [shower]. They make the men
go from the rear and the women in the front with the children. They
made the men undress in the nude in the rear and the same thing to
the women, but when they started to push them inside and beat them
and kick them that they should go inside, they all were in the same room.
Under the ceiling they had those shower heads.

About twenty-five feet away from that particular building, they had
a man-made mountain from dirt which they dug out from holes where
they used to burn the bodies. They didn't have the crematorium in the
beginning like Auschwitz had. They had holes, about four of them, which
each hole did absorb up to 10,000 people a day. The gas chamber, when
they pushed in the people there, behind that man-made mountain was
a big trailer, a black trailer, and from the trailer was hoses connected
to that building. When they piled up all the people in that room, there
was one Nazi in the front and one Nazi in the rear with a pail of lime
and they sealed off the doors. This was right in the beginning, you know,
which it wasn't so organized. But they killed people.

So when they sealed off the doors, one of the Nazis gave a signal to
somebody who was there in that trailer or whatever it is, it didn't take
a minute or so [until] the motors started to roar and evidently carbon
monoxide or whatever it was from that trailer did go into that room
through those hoses. . . . It only took minutes. [Then] they stopped the
motors. . . .

And they waited a few minutes and then to the right was an electric switch, a big electric switch. I found out, coming closer to it, that the [way the] electric switch worked is [that] inside the building were two suction fans built in on the wall and the roof had a chimney on each side, which the smell and the poison the suction fans did pull out. You can imagine when they opened up those doors, you could see the people were laying on top of each other, they were blue. For some reason or another some people had their teeth bitten into the next person's body. They must have gone through a terrible pain or God knows what, and on the wall, though they were concrete, you could see people with their fingers scratching blood on the wall. One time there were writing on the wall from blood and it did say, in Yiddish, that *der Yiden* should take *nekome*. That means that Jews should take a revenge on those murderers.

And when this was over a tractor came with trailers, two trailers, and the people used to load those bodies on those trailers like herring. Heads and heads to feet. They used to put them one over another until they loaded up and they took them to those holes that were there, and they burned them holes. . . . They gassed so many people that those holes couldn't absorb so many bodies.

Peltz was later sent to Auschwitz, where he was active in the camp resistance.

Tell me about smuggling in the camp.

We called it organizing—for stealing. It was going on, it was. Not on a big scale, but it did go on. . . . By smuggling anything you risked your life. There were people that were smuggling letters. Letters from whom to whom? Let's say this father had a daughter or a wife in the women's camp. So she wrote him a little letter and this guy did it, he did it only for pity. Didn't do it for anything. Who needed money or anything? Or if a man did write a little letter. And I happen to know a lot of people did it, and they risked their lives. If they did catch, in your possession, a piece of paper and a letter written from once place to another, this was it. Not only did they kill you, they tortured you. They wanted to know who did it and why you did it and they wanted you to tell who gave you the letter. And if you told who gave you the letter this person went to hell, too.

Some people had access to smuggle food. So he had to smuggle out something from the camp. You didn't get food for nothing. You didn't

Main Commission for the Investigation of Nazi War Crimes, Warsaw, Poland, courtesy U.S. Holocaust Memorial Museum.

Entrance gate to the Auschwitz death camp, Poland, May, 1945.

get cigarettes for nothing. You didn't get what have you for nothing. You had to smuggle out from the camp. So what did you smuggle out from the camp? Money, you didn't [have]. So you had to smuggle valuables. Where did you get the valuables? Everything was taken away. So we had prisoners, guys that they worked at the barracks where they used to sort these valuables and pack and send them to Germany. Or if you are aware, in other words, Germany, in Auschwitz, they had their own smelter. They used to take all the gold that they take away from people and make into bars. And if you talked to a lot of prisoners there they didn't even know about it. . . .

I want you to know one thing, if I may. Resistance, you're talking about resistance, probably if you heard or not that that this is documented. The Jews did try once in Birkenau, you probably heard about it, and I was present just like I'm talking to you. What did they do and what did they win? Nothing. They did machine gun eighty-four young, strong men and I had the list of it. I wish I had it today. I had the list of all eighty-four. I want you to know that I was involved in that. So what did I accomplish? They killed one German, and the German was a prisoner and he was a murderer. When they started a fire, when they did throw the gasoline on that crematorium, they did push him in alive. Big deal.

They did make a resistance. I was in the conversations a lot of times with people, especially when I do a lecture, not now as much as a few years ago, especially among young men and older persons. That they used to tell me that we did go like sheep to our death. "It wouldn't happen to me. It wouldn't happen to us." It wouldn't happen to them—baloney. I want you to know that. How in the world can you try to fight back and to resist—how can you? If your hands are tied and you can't do nothing, your mind is sick. A lot of people don't even realize that the little food that we used to get was drugged. Our minds didn't work. It happened to me, [but] as soon as I got a fair diet, or anybody, they start to organize food from the outside, the mind started to work. Every person was for himself. He tried to fight to survive every second, every hour, every day, every week. If people today can walk the streets of New York and see a man beats and stabs and kills a woman on the street and they walk and they don't even look at it and the one that look they didn't give a damn, how the heck can they call me a coward? . . . If you try to explain, they still cannot understand.

Was smuggling a form of resistance?

Yes, absolutely. Absolutely. Anything that we did was a form of resistance. . . . Some of us, we thought how in the world could it have been done to make the people aware outside in other countries of what's going on in the concentration camps, because we were under the impression the world does not know what's going on. So there were two young men. One guy was about in his late twenties, about twenty-seven or twenty-eight years old, one was about eight years younger, nine years younger, very fine two young men. And they decided to escape. Before I'm going to go any further, to escape from Auschwitz was almost impossible, especially for Jews. You had to have help from the outside. You couldn't escape, say, "Well, I'm going to take off and run away,"—no. Auschwitz and Birkenau and all the camps around and all the isolated land was some forty kilometers around. . . . If a person had help, the only way he could probably achieve an escape was if he would have a hiding place for about three, four weeks and enough food and somebody to help them and then take off, he might have a chance if somebody would come and give him a false passport and clothing and money. But those two young men, when it comes to money and some other things there was no problem—for valuables there was no problem, but the help from the outside [was difficult to get].

*Walter Peltz, Memmingen,
Germany, 1946.*

WHi3187/PZ/1/23

Auschwitz is situated in an area in Poland which it is not too far away from the Czechoslovakian border. On a clear day you could see from Auschwitz to the Carpathian Mountains. Now, from Czechoslovakia [it] is easier to go into Hungary because they border. In Hungary, at that time, had their whole Jewish population. As you probably know, Hungary was not invaded until 1944 by the Nazis, but though they had the Nazi organization in Hungary by the name of Nilosz. . . .

Those two men did plan and they did achieve and they did escape and they vanished like in the air, but not for long. . . . They did make their way through to Czechoslovakia and it took them a long time to do it. They made their way through from Czechoslovakia to Hungary, and in Hungary they got in touch with the Jewish people, whoever was in charge, to tell them what's going on, that they did escape from Auschwitz. You know what happened? They called the police and arrested them. They told them that they came here to put fear and to spread things that is not true. You know what happened to those two Jewish boys? They brought them back to Auschwitz.

You know what the Nazis did to them? I'll tell you what they did to them. First of all, they made all the Jews [watch]. They put them down on two chairs, tightened them with ropes, and they killed them. Shot them right through the temple, and they were sitting there dead for three days. This is because they risked their life and they tried to tell the world what's going on. People did not believe. To escape Auschwitz, if somebody did escape, and achieve what they did, to go into another country, this was almost impossible. How they did it is beyond me. Until today I don't know how they did it.

Peltz survived four years in the concentration camps of Majdanek, Auschwitz, Sachsenhausen, and Dachau before being liberated by the U.S. Army in May, 1945. Shortly after liberation, he married Rose Abraham, a Hungarian survivor of Dachau, and operated a clothing and yard goods store in Memmingen, Germany. The Peltzes immigrated to the United States in May, 1949, and settled in Milwaukee. Walter held a variety of jobs before becoming a partner in the Midwest Iron and Metal Company in West Allis, Wisconsin, in 1967. Rose Peltz died in 1968, and Walter married Arleen Arnstein in June, 1972. A resident of Mequon, north of Milwaukee, Peltz still works part time and lectures on the Holocaust.

*   *   *   *   *

Henry Golde

Born in Plock, Poland, on May 5, 1929, Henry Golde was the younger son of a Polish father and a Lithuanian mother.

Plock is a small provincial town, approximately 10,000 population. There were 2,000 Jews that lived there, which was a high percentage of Jews in a small town. Plock itself is a beautiful little town which lays right on the Vistula [River]. The town itself sits on a big mountain, and around the mountain there was a park and if you look at a picture of the town looking up from the Vistula, you see a very majestic church, which actually was a Catholic cathedral, and it was very very nice and picturesque. And the park was beautiful because it went all along that mountain that the town was built on.

The town itself was very clean, laid out nicely. It had its business area and it had the houses where people lived in—actually, everybody lived in apartment houses; there was no private homes like you will see here in the United States. It was typical European. The city itself had three different parks and different squares. Streets were nicely kept, and there weren't any dirt roads: they were all either cobblestones or asphalt, which was something new at the time. But the town itself was very progressive. There were three gymnasiums there, which was like a prep school, and people were mostly intellectuals. There was small industry;

there were three machine shops, which employed quite a few hundreds of people. Two of them belonged to the Jews; one was Christian. It was quite an industrious little town, where life was pretty good, I would say, as a whole for Christians and Jews.

There were also two regiments of Polish armies stationed in Plock. One was artillery, the other one was cavalry, and we had a lot of military parades, which was very cumbersome and so on. It wasn't mechanized like our army here, but they looked very beautiful on the horses and so on. I remember the times that we used to go out and there were concerts in the parks and different doings where everybody enjoyed it.

There were three sports clubs—there were two Jewish sports clubs and one Christian—and most of the Jewish young men belonged to it. They were more social than sports clubs. There were also quite a number of what you would call maybe political Zionist organizations, where a lot of young people belonged to that, too. There was always something to do in the town. Even if people would walk out and promenade town the streets and there were quite a few broadways, what you would call here in the United States, where people would walk and watch the store windows and so on. And, of course, weekends most of the people would spend just walking around the parks, which I think was very relaxing and enjoyable.

Could you tell me a little bit about your home? Had you lived there for many years?

As far as I can remember, until the beginning of the war, after the Polish-German war finished, I lived in one apartment. It was a big building, approximately eight families that lived in the building and then in the same courtyard there were three other buildings. So all in all, in the whole complex, there must have been about twenty or twenty-five families. Our apartment was a three-room apartment, which was very typical—one bedroom, one living room, and a kitchen. It was a cold apartment. We had kind of an oven, a tile oven, that went from the floor to the ceiling, which covered the whole wall, and it was fired by coal, and that was the only heat that you would have in the house. Of course, the same thing with cooking—there was a wood and coal stove in the kitchen, built right into the room, where all the cooking was done. Of course, that gave out heat too, so that was the extent of the apartment.

Where did you and your brother sleep?

Well, I slept in the same room with my parents, and my brother slept on a sort of a [pull-out] couch in the living room.

Was it unusual for a Jew to be a barber, like your father?

No, not at all, not at all. Because I remember that in Plock itself we had six or seven barber shops and quite a few young people in the trade itself. So it wasn't unusual. As a matter of fact, some people think, well, the Jews are the businesspeople, and they go into the business, where you can make money. But it wasn't so. In Poland you found Jews in every walk of life. We had carpenters in Plock and garbage collectors and practically in every trade that there was.

Did your father's customers include both Jews and non-Jews?

Yes. I would say that the majority of his trade was non-Jews. My father, actually, besides being a barber, he was kind of a doctor himself. . . . My father used to pull teeth. When a farmer came in and he had a toothache he went to a barber, and my father would pull his tooth out. If somebody had a very bad cold, he would come into the house and use some kind of a—they looked like whiskey shot glasses—and you'd smear the back of a person's back with alcohol and then you'd put the light into the glass and that glass would stick to the skin and it stays there for a while and makes a real brown mark and then you take them off, and that's supposed to take out the bad blood or whatever you call it. Everybody believed in it. I tell you quite frankly—sometimes it worked. So that's what my father was doing—a few different things. . . .

When Pilsudski died, when anti-Semitism started to flourish, I found out that I was different than the other kids. And I asked my father that question, "Why am I different? They tell me I'm different—I'm a Jew. What's a Jew?" I didn't even know at the time what a Jew, what a Christian was, and so on. And he did explain to me at length why and what and so on. Still, in my own mind, I couldn't understand, because as far as I'm concerned I have the same two eyes and one nose and two ears. And I didn't look any different—I was blond and blue-eyed and I wasn't any different than a Christian kid. "Why am I different?" "Well, you are one of the chosen people." I said, "Well, if I'm so chosen, how come that they always gang up on me and beat up on me? What did

I do wrong? I didn't do anything different than the Christian kids." My brother had to defend me. . . .

If you ask me where I can identify myself, if I'm Polish, Christian, Jew, or with the Jewish element, I would say I had mixed emotions because I did have Christian friends and I also had Jewish friends. I could not speak Yiddish, I didn't understand Yiddish, I was strictly Polish. As a matter of fact, if my father and mother talked and they didn't want us to understand, they spoke Yiddish. And they did not insist that we learn Yiddish.

How drastic were the changes after 1935?

It was very, very clear and very obvious. When Pilsudski died, a lot of radical groups came out from the woodwork, and they started intimidating Jews. As a matter of fact, they went as far as the church itself started discriminating against the Jews. There was one priest in particular that used to travel throughout the country and preach against the Jews and every time he would leave, [there] would be more or less a small pogrom on Jews, where Jewish windows were smashed in the stores and some apartments where Jews lived and Jews with beards that they caught in the streets they used to beat up and so on. So like I said, things started to happen.

Toward the time when they started talking about the war, it was so bad that all kinds of demonstrations by Christian students against the Jews happened practically every week. Newspapers openly preached against the Jews. They would put out blacklists of all the people that would trade with Jews. Student pickets were stationed at Jewish stores at various times and wouldn't allow Christians to go into Jewish stores. Signs appeared in parks, "Jews and dogs not allowed." Some Jewish couples on the Sabbath when they walked in the park were beaten up and so on. As a matter of fact, I even remember a Jewish farmer and his whole family were murdered before the war, and the police didn't even investigate the murder. So things were getting really tough and the anti-Semitism was very dominant.

Following the German occupation in September, 1939, the Golde family was ordered into ten-block Jewish ghetto of Plock.

So you left your home and moved into that area?

We lived in our apartment I would say about a month or two after the end of the [Polish-German] war. At first the order was to close all the

Jewish stores and they took all the merchandise and everything else and the Jews were out of business. And then what they had in Plock, and there was a lot of them, which they called the *Volksdeutsch*. The *Volksdeutsch* was the one that lived in Poland but he was a German national, and those were the ones that served as interpreters, as informers, for the Germans. They wore swastikas on their arms for identification and they were the most ruthless people I came across. They would start going into Jewish homes and help them search through everything. Jewish homes were looted by them, including some of the Germans in uniform.

Jews had no rights whatsoever. Rations were given out to the Jews. Jews were not allowed to go into either Polish or German stores, which even some of the Polish stores were confiscated by the Germans. The most larger stores were confiscated from the Poles and the Jews were not allowed in that. I was kind of a cocky kid. I did not wear a yellow badge because I felt nobody would recognize me. I would go into German stores, I would go into Polish stores and buy all kinds of supplies. I was more or less like a runner for a lot of neighbors because I did have blond hair and blue eyes and I felt that they wouldn't recognize me and I refused to wear yellow badges. One day I was caught. . . . Wherever you went, there were lines to buy anything; I was right in front of the line when a Polish woman pointed out to the German that was selling the milk, "He's a Jew." So she grabbed the container that I had for the milk and tipped it back into the big container and she told me to get out. And I was lucky that she just told me to get out, because if she would have grabbed me and taken me into the German headquarters I would be a dead duck because not wearing a yellow badge identifying as a Jew was a penalty of death. So I was quite lucky.

But then the order came out that all the Jews with all their possessions and furniture will move into that particular street and it's going to be a Jewish ghetto. That was only a few months after the end of the Polish-German war that the order came, and then we had to move in with other families. Each family had one room that they were allocated. We had *Judenrat*, what they call the Jewish government, that was formed by the Germans and they were the ones that were allocating rooms for Jewish families. And things were very cramped, but somehow everybody fit in that particular block. It wasn't a closed ghetto, we didn't have a wall. But leaving the ghetto by the Jew was a penalty of death. Everything was a penalty of death. If you didn't take off your hat to a German, he had the right to shoot you. Jews had no rights whatsoever. Everything was a penalty of death, and a lot of people died. . . . Right in the beginning when the Gestapo moved in, they closed the schools and they started to arrest all the intellectuals in town. Those people were never seen again.

Only Jewish intellectuals, or Polish ones as well?

Christians and Jews. They arrested the principals of high schools, principals of all the other schools, the judge, lawyers, and so on—whoever they figured are intellectuals. And apparently their thinking was, if we take away the leaders, the people will follow and will not uprise or anything like that.

> The inhabitants of the Plock ghetto were moved to the concentration camp at Mlawa, Poland, in early 1940. A week later, the Golde family, along with half the Jews of Plock, was shipped to the Jewish ghetto in Chmielnik, Poland. After six months, Golde was selected for forced labor at the munitions factory at Skarzysko-Kamienna, Poland; his parents and brother were gassed at Treblinka.

The people that were there before us must have been there for approximately six months, and you could tell right away that they weren't the only people that were there. Conditions were not good at all. There wasn't much food, the work was very hard, and the beatings and the uncertainty were great. The next day after arrival, we were chased outside in the square and the German bosses would come in and pick the people that they wanted to work in their departments. And I was put in a department where they were manufacturing blank rifle bullets. The work wasn't hard there. I was put on a machine, and I was cutting out felt to be put in the bullet so that the powder wouldn't explode like a regular bullet would. . . . As I said, the work wasn't very hard, but I started experiencing hunger, and I think that when you're hungry, your mind is not as keen as it should be. All you can think is about food, and you think mostly about survival. And it was getting progressively worse.

Every month the bosses would take everybody outside, and they would have a selection where they would select people to be eliminated, and practically every month a new transport of people would be coming in from different parts of Poland and even some from Germany. Therefore, we knew that we're going to work until we can't work anymore, and then we're going to die, because they always had replacements.

And when you see the replacements, you could see that when they came from home, the difference between the people that were in camp for a while and the newcomers that came. My feeling is that if you take a person and you don't give him any food, keep him hungry, don't give him any clothes, keep him cold, and you beat him, then you have an animal—people virtually become animals. The only concern of people was survival and how to get your stomach full. And the worst thing that happens to a person in that instance, he loses self-respect, and that's exactly what happened to the majority of the people. Some of them even lost their minds. Looking from the psychological point of view, it seemed to me that the stronger, the bigger the person was, the faster that he fell. Like you're talking about the meek will inherit the earth. To me this is very true. The survival of the person that was skinny all his life, didn't eat much—the survival of that person was much greater than the person that was big, well fed, and strong. And I've seen people, men as tall as trees, that fell like a limb. And they couldn't take it. They couldn't take the hunger, they couldn't take the beatings, they couldn't take the cold, no clothing, and the uncertainty.

The uncertainty—I think that was the worst thing that can happen to a person. You didn't know from one moment to the other what's going to happen. Life was very cheap. A person was alive one minute, the next minute he was shot, killed, beaten up, beaten to death, torn apart by dogs, and so on. Life was very, very cheap, and that's the way the Germans liked it.

Following the German evacuation of Skarzysko in the fall of 1943, Golde worked in the slave labor camp at Czestochowa for three months, spent a brief time in Buchenwald, and finally was transferred to a munitions factory at Colditz, Germany.

Tell me about your deportation to Czestochowa.

The whole camp was evacuated. The Russian front was moving into Poland and it was getting closer and closer to Skarzysko, and they decided to evacuate the camp. And that's a story in itself, too, because the German commandant come into camp and he chased everybody out in the camp square and he told everybody that he's going to make a registration, that the camp is going to be evacuated. The weak ones are going to ride on the train and the strong ones are going to march. He didn't tell us where we were going or anything like that. And the next day he came and everybody had to line up and he looked at everybody, made check marks at your name. Nobody knew what it meant, and he says the next day we're going to be evacuated. He came the next day, and they chased everybody out again and the German commandant started calling the names out. And when I saw the people that he was calling up I knew those people that are going to ride are not going to ride very far, because they were weak, they were the old ones, and so on. And then when he called my name, I didn't appear.

But the point where I knew that something is happening is because he wasn't waiting for anybody to show up, he was calling out the names and soon as he had fifty people, they were marched outside camp right away. And I said, no, those people are not going to ride. What do I do? I knew that he's not going to end that because people were getting smarter. They knew what it meant, and he had less and less people that were showing up. I said I have to hide, but where do you hide? They're going to look in the barracks and under the barracks and everything else. And then it dawned on me. There was a hospital barrack in the corner of the camp and when somebody died in camp or in the hospital they would take the body out and throw it behind the barrack on the pile and when the pile was big then they would come with a truck and load the bodies on the truck and take them away for burial, I suppose. And I said, that's the place to hide. They're never going to look there that day. And I started moving out of the ranks and there was still a big chaos because the Jewish police were chasing everybody out from the barrack still, and I circled around and I found myself behind that hospital barracks and I seen a big pile of bodies and I lay down among the bodies and I lay there a whole day, and that's how I saved my life.

I heard the shots, I heard the screaming and dogs barking and so on. When it got quiet at the end of the day, it was getting dark, I got out and I joined everybody else, and I realized then that half of the camp was gone. And the men that were left—men and women, actually— were telling the story of what happened, how they were taking everybody and shooting them on the spot.

How did you get to Buchenwald?

It happened exactly the same as what happened in Skarzysko. Apparently the front was moving again and the Russians were getting close and they got us out. They put everybody, both camps, on a train in closed boxcars and they took us to Buchenwald.

How did Buchenwald differ from the other camps you were in?

In Buchenwald, at that time, there was no work. Buchenwald actually was a political concentration camp where you found people from different nationalities for different reasons. There was a lot of Germans, communist Germans, murderers, different kind of prisoners. There was a lot of gypsies, there were German Jews, there were Frenchmen, there were Poles, and there was also a small [number of] American prisoners-of-war, and there was also an English prisoner-of-war camp. And of course their conditions were completely different from ours. And each nationality, each crime, in Buchenwald was marked different, like German Communists would wear red badges on their uniforms. . . .

The only time that the Germans would come into camp was to count the people, and they did that twice a day. You died of boredom. And you seen people and that's the first place that I've seen the walking dead. And you would ask yourself what were the walking dead? They were the people that were dead, who looked like skeletons, but apparently their body didn't lie down yet. Their minds were gone, they wandered around blindly, they actually were dead, but they still walked around. Buchenwald was worse, as far as I'm concerned, than any other work camp because at least when you were working you might forget a little bit about all the other troubles like food, hunger, and cold, and so on. When you're not doing anything, you might die from boredom. And you think more of the things that are essential to survive. That's why a lot of people died. . . .

The most interesting thing that happened when we arrived there, first of all, what we've seen, first of all we heard the dogs bark. When they opened the doors on the trains, when you were in Buchenwald, and there was a big sign on the front gate which said, "Arbeit Macht Frei," which means work makes you free. And when we marched in the band was playing, a band of inmates, and everything was done nice and proper, and we had to march. That was a huge camp, there were thousands and thousands of people. There was a big chimney, and on top of that chimney it says, "The only way out of here is through this chimney." And we knew that was a crematorium. And also there was gas chambers there, too. When we arrived, there were different prisoners that were walking around among the newcomers, the new transports, and asking—and there were two men in particular—asking people who was a Jewish policeman, who was an overseer, who was acting bad towards other Jews, and naturally they were pointed out and they were given a death sentence by committee of prisoners, and most of those who did any atrocities died there. Either they reported themselves to be put in gas chambers or they found them hanging themselves and so on. They beat them half senseless. . . .

Henry Golde, May, 1946.

WHi(X3)50177

And you got kind of used to the sign [on the chimney]. You got kind of used to the saying—yes, it's true, there's no way out of here. But I was lucky again. [After] being a couple of months there an order came that such and such people to report for work that were going to be evacuated to a different camp, and I was one of them. And apparently, the people that worked in Camp C in Skarzysko-Kamienna were the ones that were picked to go to a different factory, and we were put on a train again and we arrived in a suburb of Leipzig, Colditz, where they had a factory that were manufacturing the parts for the flying bombs that the Germans had that they were sending to England. They were very dreaded piece of equipment that the Germans devised which the British at the time or even the Americans didn't have no answer for. In that particular factory they were only were doing one part of it. They were making different parts in different places so nobody got wise.

Golde and the other slave laborers at Colditz were marched to the concentration camp at Theresienstadt in Czechoslovakia, where they were liberated by the Russian army on May 1, 1945. Golde remained at Theresienstadt for another month until the British government flew him and

300 other youths to Windermere, England, where he was trained as a tailor. In 1948 he married Mali Lipshitz, and four years later the Goldes immigrated to the United States.

How did you feel when you saw the Statue of Liberty?

We did not arrive at Ellis Island like the refugees did. We docked at the harbor in New York and going through customs we were treated the same as any other passenger that would be coming over here. It was quite a sight when I saw the skyline of New York and the Statue of Liberty. I can't explain the feeling, but it made me feel so far removed from where I came from, the war, and I had a feeling of safety where I did not have it in England, maybe because of the closeness of being in Europe, to what happened during the war. Maybe I felt that I cannot be touched here by another war. The memory was still fresh of the Nazis and so on, and the nightmares that I had after the war of what happened, but that feeling left me when we arrived in New York.

The Golde family lived in New York, Pennsylvania, and Ohio before arriving in Wisconsin in 1954. Henry held various sales and tailoring jobs in Milwaukee, Delavan, Merrill, and Appleton prior to his retirement in 1994. Henry and Mali Golde had two children before divorcing in 1964. Henry then married Marie Roethke in 1967, and the couple had a son prior to their 1992 divorce. Golde currently lives in Appleton, where he speaks in schools about his Holocaust experiences.

*   *   *   *   *

Rosa Goldberg Katz

Rachel (Rosa) Goldberg was born in Lodz, Poland, on May 6, 1924, to a financially comfortable liberal Jewish family.

Tell me about anti-Semitism when you were growing up.

Eastertime, for instance, they used to have religious demonstrations, parades, carrying the Madonna and all that and flags and singing religious songs. And with that they never missed to shout "Death to the Jews," "Jews to Palestine," stuff like that. And this always kind of bothered me just terribly. Then one time, I will never forget it, it was May 3 when there were all kind of demonstrations. This was a national holiday, and there were parades. All the schools took part in it, Jewish children too, with flags and you name it, the whole bit. We were always the last

WHi3187/KZ/1/3

Rosa Goldberg's family, Lodz, Poland, 1934: (l. to r.) Sara (mother), Rosa, Hersh (uncle), Moishe (brother), and Abraham (father).

ones in the parade, never mixed, always the last one. Jewish people were attacked all the time. One time I remember, I never forget it. A whole bunch of gentiles came into our courtyard and they were pushing some people around. And there were a couple young men kind of stood up to them, and it was just terrible. Not a policeman in sight. Blood was just gushing all over. So many people were hurt. This was before the war.

Did you identify yourself as a Pole, as a Jew, or as a Polish Jew?

I often question that. Even now, if somebody asked me where are you from—naturally, because how can I hide my accent? I never say I'm Polish or Jewish. I say Jewish, this is my religion. I was born in Poland. I never say I'm Polish; I always say I was born in Poland. I don't want that. At work I have a lot of contacts with gentile people, in fact mostly gentile people and no problems at all. I suppose they don't know I'm Jewish. If they ask me, I gladly tell them what I am. But it never came up, just "From where are you from?" So my answer is always [that] I was born in Poland. I never say I'm Polish.

How would you have answered that question before the war?

That's a good question. I probably would say I'm a Jew, because we weren't accepted as first-class citizens as anybody else. Actually we had the same rights. We were I don't know how many generations in Poland. Here in this country, first-generation, second-generation, they are Americans. Someone asks me, "Where are you from?" I'm from Oshkosh. I'm American, I'm an American citizen. I feel I'm an American. But in Poland they never let us be that way. We were second-grade citizens.

Naturally, the Jewish men went into the army, but they were treated just terrible. They were made fun, they were given the worst jobs. Or there was never a Jewish policeman. There were a lot of doctors, but they never studied in Poland. People who could afford to send their children probably to Austria, France, or England—a lot of them went to England to study. In Krakow there was a huge university. It was just terrible for the Jewish students who went there. Every other day somebody had a concussion from being beaten up. This was before Hitler.

In November, 1939, two months after the Germans occupied Lodz, Rosa Goldberg, her parents, and her brother were moved into the Jewish ghetto, where they shared a two-room apartment with eight other people.

What did you take with you?

I don't even remember—probably clothes. There were so many neighborhoods they just came in and they just chased the people out during the night, so I remember several nights I slept [with] several dresses on, just in case they come during the night so we have some change of clothing with us. We slept in our coats, in our shoes, with a bag right next to the bed in case if they come in the middle of the night we just grab the bags and have the clothing what we had on. I remember I had three, four, five—I don't even remember, I could hardly move—clothes on me. Everybody else did that. . . .

[After moving into the ghetto,] my father was very, very depressed. My [parents] were losing weight and looked like skeletons. The food wasn't enough to live on and not enough to die with—just torture. Everybody was always hungry. People swelled up from hunger. Then some soup kitchens opened up. Somebody spilled some soup on the street, people would stop and look at the soup, "Oh my, look at the soup. It's wasted." Next to that spill could be somebody lying dying.

They didn't feel sorry for the poor wretched person who's dying there, but they were sorry for the soup. What hunger can do to human beings, it's unbelievable.

And they kept coming in—they kept sending in people. We were so overcrowded, just terrible. No hospitals, no medical supplies, no doctors. Maybe there were doctors, but nobody knew who is the doctor, where the doctors are. Every so often, they kept shipping people from Czechoslovakia, people from Germany. A lot of people came in. It was amazing. We couldn't believe our eyes.

Apparently Hitler was studying the backgrounds of a lot of people in Germany. Some of the people who came into the ghetto, were sent into the ghetto, apparently some ancestor far, far, way back must have been a Jew and they were considered also Jews and they were sent into our ghetto. Some of them actually came in Nazi uniforms. They were members of the Nazi party. They never even knew that somebody, some great-great-grandparents or somebody way back was a Jew. They never knew about it until Hitler found it out for them. It was ironic—they came in with Nazi uniforms.

How were they treated?

Not very nice, I'm sure, I'm sure. All of a sudden they changed the ghetto to a labor camp. They started organizing tailor shops to make uniforms for the army and, I think, shoes and all kind of factories, all of a sudden. There were factories in that place; they just put them to use. They organized it for different things they needed for the army. And this somehow saved us probably, my father especially, because he was an engineer with special machineries and they had just maybe three or four men in the whole ghetto who could do this type of work and they needed him. So my dad had permission to go from place to place, and he also managed somehow to get me a job, and if you worked you were safe, because they kept coming in taking streets and just deporting people. I don't know what they did with them—other labor camps or maybe concentration camps.

We didn't know anything about concentration camps, just that they would come into our block in just middle of the night and shouting, shooting with machine guns, with horrible voices, "Raus, Juden! Raus, raus, Schweinehund! [Get out, Jews! Get out, get out, swine!]," swearing, and people just walked out of their houses—from their beds, really—in their nightgowns and piled on the buses. They took babies away from the mothers' arms and just put them on the buses and nobody ever saw

Courtesy Yad Vashem.

Deportation of Jews from the Lodz ghetto, 1942.

them again. And they made lists of children. Parents disappeared and then there were children without parents, so right away people organized, somebody got to take care of the children. So they opened homes just like orphanages, and then they opened places for people who were sick, like hospitals. All of a sudden the doctors came out from hiding, and they were helping. We had to help each other because we didn't get any help from nobody, especially from the Polish people, from the gentiles. You would think they would help their own people, but they didn't consider us as Polish citizens even though we were there I don't know how many generations. . . .

At one time they sent in some horse meat [to the ghetto]. Naturally, most of the Jews were Orthodox, and this wasn't kosher. Mother insisted that Father and my brother and I, we should eat it. She prepared it, but she wouldn't touch it. And she was starved, half starved. She cooked it and prepared it. She wanted to save her family. She insisted that the children eat it, and my dad, but she wouldn't. Finally, we made her eat because we were afraid for her. We said, "If you won't eat, we won't eat," and this kind of made her eat.

And I remember that the rabbi, main rabbi in the ghetto, called the people together. A lot of people didn't want to touch the meat, and they were starved and he told them—I remember it was in the middle of a square with benches, like a little park, and he asked the people to come there. . . . And whoever could walk, whoever could get out of bed to come there, they did. And he told them, "If you want to live to eat kosher again, you better eat that horse meat." He gave them the blessing. And I think a lot of people did eat after that. . . .

I really don't know how we survived four and a half years in the ghetto. It's a mystery. Not many did, actually. People just dropped like flies. They went to bed and never got up. Whole families went to bed and all of a sudden you don't see them, you went there to check on them and they were all dead in bed.

What about disease?

Terrible. There were a lot of TB, sickness. My youngest uncle, my mother's youngest brother—he was same age as my oldest sister—he died. He got TB and within a week he was dead. Mostly people died out of hunger. . . . And all of a sudden the ghetto wasn't overcrowded anymore. . . .

In 1942 they kept coming and getting people out of bed and taking children away and so on. In 1942 we had to get out again on our block on our street where we lived, our section, and they were picking people at random. People could hardly walk. They couldn't even lift their feet up to climb on a big, huge truck, and they piled them in like cattle. I think it was in July, 1942, my brother and I and my parents went out, and they picked my mom and my father. And whoever screamed or made a noise they took them, too. They stood there with those big, huge rubber things hitting the people to climb on those trucks, and I saw my mom being pushed and my father being hit. He was trying to help my mother to get up, and I started to scream, and my brother and another neighbor pushed me down so they wouldn't notice me and my brother just put his hand on my mouth. If they would have heard me, they would have taken me too. I don't know how my parents got on the truck, and all of a sudden I see my mother and father just waving to us from the truck.

This was the last time I saw my mother. But my father came back because somebody told us, "You better go get that manager, from that factory, tell them that they took your father." And so my brother and I, we . . . went and they got him back. . . . They got my dad out. They found my father. There were people, hundreds of them, just piled in in tiny rooms and trying to put them on the wagons and ship them someplace. Then we heard shooting. God knows what they did. Somehow the Germans found my dad and brought him home. But trying to find Mother—[my parents] were separated. With all the turmoil and all that confusion and screaming and crying they were separated, and father came back, but not my mother. And this was the last time I saw her.

This was 1942, and from then on, every day they took people away. We didn't know where they were shipping them. Didn't know anything about them. We just knew that people just disappeared. My cousins we lived with—they took their children at the same time when they took my mom and father. And this was just terrible. After my mom was gone my brother met a girl and he married her, so he moved out too. So there were just the four of us in that apartment. . . .

Every day my father had a piece of bread, because I realized if I don't do that, I won't be able to keep him. We still had hope. We never lost our faith, our hope. I questioned a lot, how come God allows all that. I was very bitter, naturally. Who wouldn't be? But I felt I have to take over now. I wasn't the daughter, I was the parent to my father, because I got to keep him alive, and I did until 1944, until 1944. When was it? August, I think. That's when the war was going bad for the Germans already and the Russians were coming closer, so they liquidated the ghetto. So I think it was August 1944 that they were shipping transports. We knew they were liquidating.

My brother and his wife, those two were intellectuals, they're going to fight back. They're going to hide. We realized something is happening, something's going on. Where do they ship all those people? What are they doing with all those people? We knew that they're doing something with them, but we didn't know anything about concentration [camps] or Auschwitz or anything—at least I didn't. Anyway, finally, the factories were still going, my father was still going to work. I was, too. My brother was, my sister-in-law was.

Courtesy Yad Vashem.

Deportation of Jews from the Lodz ghetto, ca. 1940–1944.

Finally, at one time they liquidated the part where we were living. We were supposed to go someplace else because there was nobody left where we were. The people were gone, disappeared. So we moved in with my uncle and there were several families together again, deciding what to do. In the meantime one of my aunts had the baby with the uncle who died. They took one child away and she got pregnant again in the ghetto and she had another baby. This was just terrible to see those little babies, the way they were dragged away from their mothers' arms. . . . They had dogs, wild dogs. They took babies away from the mothers and just threw them in the air, and they were shooting at them. When the babies dropped down onto the ground, the dogs tore them apart. Stuff like that.

Finally, my sister-in-law and my brother decided they were going to hide because [we thought] the Russians are [close]. . . . They decided they were going to stick it out, they're going to hide in the ghetto. We saw those wagons, those cattle wagons where they would pile the people in. They're not going to be shipped like this. So it was just my father and I. For a week we didn't hear from my brother and his wife. We didn't know. And my sister-in-law's mother was with them, too. We didn't know what's happened. All of a sudden they decided they just couldn't hide. There was not enough food and they were suffocating. I don't know where they were hiding, some attic, I don't know. We got together again, and what do we do? So we decide we're just going to go; you couldn't stay. My uncles decided the same thing—they're going to go. . . . So we just took a whatever was left and we walked to those wagons and we were shipped to Auschwitz.

Who were you with?

My father, my sister-in-law, my brother, and my sister-in-law's mother.

And when you got to Auschwitz that was the last time you saw any of them?

This was the last time I saw my father and my brother. We were separated right away. But I was with my sister-in-law.

What was your arrival at Auschwitz like?

It was absolutely bewildering. All of a sudden the train stops and the doors open. It was daytime and it blinded us after so long being in the dark. We couldn't see for I don't know how long. I couldn't focus on anything. The only thing we could hear was horrible shouting in German, swearing at us, pushing. There was, "Move here, move there." I was just like a robot. And all of a sudden my eyes got adjusted to the daytime, to the light, and I realized when we arrived that there were hundreds of people out of those wagons and there were soldiers with dogs and machine guns, pushing here, pushing there, screaming. People crying, people being kicked, people being beaten. It was such a bewildering feeling, and I kept saying, "Where are we? What's going on? What's happened?" It was just like you dream, and you're trying to wake up. I kept saying, "No, this must be a nightmare. I'm going to wake up any minute, and this is not happening at all." That kind of feeling—very bewildering. You didn't know what was going on.

We saw barracks, huge barracks, but fences first, miles and miles of fences. And finally they told us to get out, to line up, men here, women here, and all of a sudden I realized that my brother and my father went in one direction and Hela, my sister-in-law, and her mother and I went in a different direction, and I realized we won't being seeing each other anymore. We are being separated.

And it just so happened I picked up a little suitcase—we had our last piece of bread in it, and I ran out and grabbed the bread out of the suitcase and I ran to my dad and I gave it to him. And I was pushed right back to the women's line. I could tell my dad was terribly nervous, because they were marching. There was so much going on, so much shouting and shooting and screaming and crying. It's unbelievable. I cannot describe it. A horrible nightmare is not as horrible as what was going on then. This was Auschwitz. All of a sudden I knew my dad knew what was going on, and he started breaking his bread, and he was giving to this man and this man. "To share that bread because this is the last piece of bread I will ever eat"—somehow I felt that's what my father was thinking of here. He did it in such a nervous way. He was a very calm man, very intelligent and very thoughtful man. He always thought to honor live things. He was a thinking man. I knew by the way he was breaking that bread, he knew that something terrible was going to happen to all of us. And he said, "Let's eat that bread. Everybody should have a piece of that bread."

And we were marched in different directions. And we came in, Hela and her mother and I, we were just holding on like for dear life so we won't be separated. Then they took Hela's mother away in a different line, probably the older people.

Courtesy Yad Vashem.

Lines of men and women after separation at Auschwitz, 1944.

This was a selection?

A selection. And Hela and I were just hanging onto each other, shaking. Then they marched us into a huge building and they told us to get undressed, strip all our clothes, and then came soldiers in and out, in and out, pushing us around like we were cattle, not human beings. And then they told us we're going to take a shower. We didn't know—a shower is a shower. But then they did select some people for a different shower— anyway, we went into a shower. Apparently it was the right shower. It wasn't the gas shower. But we didn't see Hela's mother anymore. Hela was very upset, and so was I.

Then they shaved our heads. They were spraying us with all kinds of—I don't know what they were spraying us with. And finally we were done. While they were shaving my head, somebody else was shaving Hela's head, and I realized that Hela is not near me and I realized we were separated. Finally, they let us go out, because somebody else was in line and we were supposed to go out a different door to a hallway. And I kept looking around, "Hela, Hela," calling. And then somebody next to me is calling, "Rushka, Rushka"—it's Rose, little Rose, in Polish—and all of sudden we looked at each other. It was Hela, standing right next to me, and I didn't recognize her. She had beautiful long hair, braids almost to her very waistline. She was a beautiful girl. Everybody admired her hair. It was thick, black, real black hair. We looked at each other. She was calling me and looking for me, and I was looking [for her]. We were standing next to each other and we didn't recognize each other, naked and without hair. Can you imagine that? No, nobody can. And we looked at each other, and with all the tragedy, with tears in our eyes, we started laughing.

And then they marched us off to a different place and there were lying piles and piles of clothing. We had to leave all our luggage, everything. They checked our teeth for gold fillings or whatever, and I suppose some people maybe who had [fillings] maybe they pulled it or taken someplace else. I don't know what they did, but I'm sure they did just that. Then we had to leave all our clothes in a big pile and they gave us those horrible Auschwitz uniforms with the stripes. It was almost ridiculous. A tall person got a short dress; a tiny little person had a long dress. It was just absolutely unbelievable.

And we were pushed around again, marched up again to the barracks. This was something else again. We had to sleep just lined up like sardines, actually like sardines in a can, one person on the top of the other. I was lying between the legs of somebody else and somebody else was lying on top of me. That's the way we slept, one next to the other.

In the morning we were rushed out—the *Kapos* [prisoners in charge of other prisoners in a concentration camp], they were with horrible shriek[ing] voices. Those were Jewish people. They rushed us out. This was our first night. It was just terrible. It was so hot, still was in August. The barracks were locked, no windows, and you piled on top of each other. People were crying, people were hysterical. Some people were sick, some people had diarrhea right on the top of each other. Some people had nightmares; I don't think anybody had ever had a nightmare like this. This was indescribable. You can read a million books and see a million movies [and] it's still not the way. You cannot describe it. And if somebody cried, they were hit. The *Kapo* was hitting them—not only the person who cried, but the people next to them. So everybody was watching out for each other, not to move, not to turn, not to do anything. You just lie like sardines, literally, like sardines in a can. That's the way we were lying there, all night long.

In the morning they chased us out of the barracks again, early, the crack of dawn. And this is the northern part of Poland, which gets really cold at night but very hot during the day at that time of the year. We didn't have shoes; somehow I managed somehow to get two left shoes, mind you, which killed my feet. We had to stand out in line; they were counting us. We had to stay there I don't know for how long. People were just fainting. We had to stay. First the *Kapo* counted, then some German women came and counted, and then somebody else came and counted. I don't know why they wanted to count us. They knew what they had there.

And then they wanted us to wash in another barrack which was just a little faucet. The water wasn't running, just dripping. Hundreds of people just managing, barely managing to wet your hands. How can you wash that way? Pushing and shoving. Some girls had their periods, blood just running down their legs, nothing to clean, no nothing, no pads, not even a rag. Then there were selections again. They took us to a different place, a distance away from our barracks, where we were staying. We had to get undressed again—it was another selection. Hela, my sister-in-law, she had pleurisy in the ghetto. She was sick, and so she had a little scar where she had a drainage of the fluids from her lungs. She still had a little scar on the side of her chest, and all of a sudden we realized if somebody wasn't perfect on their body, they took them away. So it was a feeling that I was afraid for Hela because of that little scar she had on her chest. So I told Hela, "Let's change places," so I could be out of line and somehow cover her scar with my shoulder or something like that. And the German noticed what I was trying to do, that I was a little bit out of line. With his fists, he just pushed me back, but somehow I realized I've got to save Hela and I just managed to fall this way, so they never noticed that she had that scar. They picked some people out, probably older people, and the rest were marched back to the same barracks. . . .

I think [we were there for] about ten days, then out again, shouts and screaming and shooting with the machine guns, always machine guns. They marched us up someplace. They marched us off to a field right next to where we arrived, where the crematoriums were, and they told us to wait on that field right next to the crematorium. . . . We looked at our arms—we didn't get any number. Usually for the people who didn't get the numbers, [if] they didn't bother to give a number, we were destined for the ovens. We didn't care—faster the better, sooner the better.

They must have forgotten about us because wagons kept rolling in night and day continuously, and the ovens, the smoke was going from those ovens. The smell, it was just terrible. During the day we were lying with no food, no water. It must have been about forty-eight hours we were lying in that field like they'd forgotten. They had completely forgotten about us. Apparently that's what happened because they were so busy with so many transports coming in with people and crying and screaming—you could hear night and day. It never stopped. It never stopped. They were so busy burning those poor, poor, wretched people.

All of a sudden a bunch of Germans came and told us, shouting and screaming—they always shouted, always shouted in German their horrible swear words. Called us all the lowest of the lowest names to get up and "Schweinehund [swine]"—terrible words—to line up again and marched us off. We didn't know where, we thought this is it. All of a sudden you realize what was going on in Auschwitz. We were lying next to the crematoriums. They were packing us into wagons again and the wagons were just terrible. Apparently they were transporting in those wagons [it] must have been flour, [because] it was all white, white dust, and others had coal dust in them. They packed us all in those wagons and they closed it and all of a sudden we were moving. We were riding again. We didn't know what was going on. They were taking us from Auschwitz.

[We had] no idea where we were going. . . . After a day or so, we felt like the train stopped and we felt a moving here and back and forth like detaching certain wagons and changing tracks or whatever. Later on I figured out that's what it was. Then our train was moving again, oh, about another day. And finally we came in and all of a sudden the doors were opened and out in the daylight again, and we looked and we came to a station in a beautiful city. Then all of a sudden we notice someplace it says Berlin—Berlin, Germany.

And they told us to get out from the wagons and we were just a sight. First of all, our heads were shaven. People who were in the coal wagons were just black with black dust, dirty. The ones who were in the other one—I don't know what it was, flour or some kind of white material there. They looked like ghosts, you know, all white with white dust, and the dresses, the prison dresses they gave us—the tall person had the short dress, the short person had the long dress. We looked just like a masquerade, really, if it wouldn't have been so tragic. We looked at each other, and we actually laughed, we looked so funny. We had those toilet buckets on the wagons, and they told us to remove it and carry this with us.

And all of a sudden we realized we are in Berlin and Berlin has been *Judenrein* [Jew-free] I don't know for how many years. All of a sudden we were marching on the streets, beautiful clean, beautiful Berlin, beautiful boulevards and streets and everything. Beautiful city. And the German people, they stopped and looked—what is this? There you're looking shaven, they didn't know if you were a man or woman because we were all shaven heads, carrying those buckets. . . . Somehow we managed to get the message from one person to another, "We are in

Berlin, did you know?" We were about 500 Jewish women—"I bet you anything they don't even know they got 500 Jews there all of a sudden and Berlin is *Judenrein,* and here they got 500 dirty Jews on the top of everything." And they used to call us dirty Jews, but we were literally dirty, coming from Auschwitz and staying in those wagons. All of a sudden we said, "Let's leave a souvenir. I don't know if we're going to be staying here or not." We were moving those buckets and spilling it all over Berlin. This was the funny part and somehow it made us laugh. I forgot that I could laugh. And all of a sudden for the first time I don't know in how long I started to laugh. Just the thought of it—we are spilling all that mess all over the beautiful Berlin, spotless, clean Berlin streets.

And they brought us into barracks. Just coming from Auschwitz, it was heaven. Bunks, bunk beds, but first we had to have showers. There were showers galore. Must have been about ten, fifteen showers in that place. Naturally, the clothes had to be thrown away, it was so filthy and dirty. For [the past] ten days nobody could wash, and it was just indescribable how we looked, just indescribable. We didn't look like humans at all. . . . There were ten showers and we were about maybe 200 per barrack. There were three barracks, I think, and we were showering continuously, just to get that smell out of our system from Auschwitz. I still could smell Auschwitz. Doesn't matter how many times I washed and scrubbed myself, almost fanatically, I still could smell Auschwitz, the ovens and the dirt and the filth. It was just almost fanatically I scrubbed. Day and night everybody was in the showers.

The food was edible, and somehow we got the strength back. Somehow we feel it was a different atmosphere. But it was still a mystery—what are we going to be doing here? We knew that we are not as so much in danger as we were in Auschwitz. We knew that we here for a purpose, but we didn't know what are we going to be doing. Nobody told us anything because no German came near us because we were in quarantine. I think it was about two weeks [later], or maybe a little longer, finally some big shot German, a huge, huge guy, and we recognized some of the soldiers who were with us with the trains, came out again, count again. I don't know why they were counting all the time, all the time counting. And then there was somebody else with a booklet and they were trying to take names. Later on we figured it out. We were all in a big transport, and [on] that transport from Auschwitz there were about 500 French women, and the French women were supposed to have gone to Berlin to work for Krupps. So apparently the officer who was in charge of that transport made a mistake. Instead of the French people, the wagons with the French people, he took the wagons of us, the Polish Jewish women. The French women went with the other people. . . .

Now the funny part comes. The Germans didn't know that we were Jews. They took it for granted that they ordered French women and that's what they got—listen to that, "ordered" French slaves. They called us slaves, *Häuptlinge*. So that big officer, almost like he treated us like we were soldiers, sound off, the name. First of all, he was trying to talk to us in German, then he realized that maybe we don't understand what he was saying, which most of us did, because knowing Yiddish is pretty similar. Then he asked if there's anybody who could speak German between us. There was a couple girls—she was from Czechoslovakia, but she also could speak German, so she raised her hand. Okay. So he told her to tell us that we going to be working at Krupps. First of all he wants to have all the names. So okay, fine. So the first person, what's your name? There was a Goldberg, there was a Rosenstein, there was a Rosenblatt and then all of a sudden he stopped. And we could tell.

Probably a blood vessel must have busted in his head because his head turned purple. He realized we are not Germans, but who has Rosenberg and Goldberg—Jews. And he asked us, "What are you?" So the translator said, "We are all Jewish women." And he called the officer who was in charge and he took out his gun with the barrel, and he started hitting him over the head right in front of us and kicking him and swearing. We stood there watching a German being beaten. Can you imagine what this meant? This was one of our little revenges. Actually I could say that. And it was funny. It took so much effort on our part not to start laughing. We were just holding onto each other on the knees and squeezing our hands to each other and saying, "My gosh, it was worth waiting for that." To realize that it was a big mistake then and that probably would have cost them, if the other, higher officers, would find out that instead they brought 500 Jews into Berlin, Berlin, *Judenrein* Berlin, [the officers] would probably be sent to the Russian front. I'm sure some of them did go right away—from then we never saw them again.

Apparently they were afraid to let anybody know who we were, so they just left it alone. This probably saved our lives. Left us alone and gave us a big speech that we're going to be working at Krupps, and we have to work hard if we want to stay here, if we want to be surviving, otherwise we going to be sent back to concentration camps. He gave us a whole spiel, and they gave us clean clothes, changes, and they left. That's the way we came to Berlin, by pure mistake. . . .

But then something else started—the bombardment.

Did the bombers hit the plant where you worked?

Several times, but not bad. We still could work in it. The next day, a terrible night of bombing, and they counted us, again counting. Nobody was missing, we were all there. All of a sudden the Germans were calling us the devil, *Teufels*, because nothing ever happened. And many of the Germans we worked with, many times you realized they're not there. They never came back, probably because [they] were hit wherever they were living.

Towards the end they allowed us to go down in the shelter. If there was a raid during the day and we were at the factory, they let us go into the shelter. But not completely down—a higher level of the shelter. Apparently they had several levels. And you know, some of the Germans actually didn't go down, they stayed on the same level we were. I bet you anything they probably believed if they're going to be with us nothing will happen, because there were so many raids, so many bombings, and we were all accounted for and [the bombs] never hit our barracks. Maybe the Americans or the British knew where the barracks were, I don't know. It's a possibility. Sometimes we had to cover our faces with blankets, which I never did.

The funniest thing—I wasn't even afraid. I kept sitting watching the skies lit up with all those lights from the bombs, the reflections. First they threw lights down so they could light up the area so they can see where to drop the bombs. It almost looked like a Christmas tree with all the lights in the sky. I actually enjoyed it. I was under the same bombs, it could have hit us too, but I was not afraid. I kept saying, "Come on, more, send them down more, more bombs, more bombs. Let them have it." This was my revenge, really. I'm not a revengeful person, but in this case I feel whatever it was dished out to them it wasn't enough.

Goldberg assembled timing mechanisms for German bombs during the next eight months. In March, 1945, she and her sister-in-law were shipped to the concentration camp at Ravensbrück, Germany. The Swedish Red Cross liberated the camp a month a later, and Goldberg was sent to Sweden.

Would you describe your liberation by the Red Cross?

This was just something beautiful, but we didn't realize what was going on. We did not know what's happening. All of a sudden we were called out again, counted again, lined up again, and marched off someplace. And all of a sudden there was somebody taking, they wanted to have all our names. In Berlin we had a number. My number was 389, I think, if I remember right. And it was so many years until anybody asked my name except close friends, and all of a sudden, even the close friends, we didn't call each other by name, we were just zombies. All of a sudden somebody's taking our names down. It took me about five minutes to think of my name. What is my name? I gave her my number from Berlin. "No, I want your name—your last name, your first name." I stood there for about five minutes, thinking "What is my name?" Finally, it came to me. I gave her my name. We still didn't know what was going on. Nobody told us anything. We thought, "Oh boy, probably this is it. This is the end." By that time we knew about the ovens, word got around. But we didn't care. Whatever should happen, just to get it over with. They couldn't do anything to us anymore. We had no feelings, no fear, nothing, just nothing. Just a sack of bones, really—no flesh anymore, but bones. To do something to human beings like that.

And then we waited again, waited again, and then all of a sudden buses start coming into the camp. Soldiers in uniforms ran out from those buses and they were kind of herding us real fast, "Hurry up, hurry up, hurry up. Let's go in." Pushing us in those buses and taking off in a hurry. We didn't know what was going on. Those were the Swedish Red Cross buses. We thought they were German officers—they were wearing uniforms. You didn't see swastikas, but some of the soldiers didn't wear always swastikas. We didn't look that hard. We saw soldiers and buses, they're taking us someplace. But the buses were nicer. They were ambulances. And then we were flying and those people, some of them, could speak German. They were trying to explain it, but we were not capable to comprehend what they were talking to us. And they had food there, but when the soldiers, the Swedish Red Cross soldiers, looked at us, they were afraid to give us the food, because they knew we were sick, we were all sick from those Red Cross packages. The only thing they let us have was water, sips of water, because they must have been trained in that coursework or first aid type of work probably. They realized we couldn't have anything solid because we were so bad off.

And then we were just flying through one city after another and at night all of a sudden we heard airplanes above us and there was some bombing. They were bombing us on the way. Later on we know the story how this came about. Himmler made that pact with Folke Bernadotte.[2] He wanted an affidavit from Folke Bernadotte that he saved

---

[2] Folke Bernadotte (1895–1948) was a Swedish statesman and Red Cross representative. In March and April, 1945, he negotiated with Heinrich Himmler and secured the release from concentration camps of more than 7,000 Scandinavians, including 4,000 Danish Jews held at Theresienstadt. He also arranged for the release of 10,000 women, 2,000 of them Jews from various countries, from Ravensbrück. Most of these women were then evacuated to Sweden.

WHi3187/KZ/1/11

Hela Goldberg, Bernard Katz, and Rosa Goldberg Katz,
Vegby, Sweden, April, 1948.

5,000 or whatever the number was, Jewish people because the war was almost over. He wanted to save his back. This way that he was the good one. He saved all those people from camp. And probably somebody else found out, and that's why they were bombing us. During the night we were hiding in the woods and then during the daytime we were running.

We made it to the border, to Denmark, and then when we came to Denmark, we didn't go into the city. Right by the border they had barracks put up, and the tables were just piled with food, all kind of food, but who could eat? We slept in barns with hay on it because who knows what kind of disease we had after all those years in camp. The Danish people, then they saw us in our condition, and they were crying just looking at us. And they couldn't be kinder, but what could they do? They were afraid to keep us there too long because after all that bombing some people were injured. They were kept in Denmark—they had to be taken to the hospital in Denmark.

We stayed there overnight, and then we went to Copenhagen. And oh, the people were greeting us on the railroad stations with flags and trying to give us cigarettes, trying to give us food. We weren't even able to reach out and take any cigarettes, but we could see their kindness, their fear, the way we looked in the uniforms we had on, and the way we looked. It was just horror and we could see their horror and then we realized then we must look like a fright. And from there we went on a boat and across to Malmo.

Goldberg worked as a tailor in Sweden until March, 1948, when she married Bernard Katz, also a survivor. The couple immigrated to the United States the following month and lived in Statesville, North Carolina, before moving to Oshkosh, Wisconsin, in 1953. The couple had two sons and two daughters before Rosa returned to school and received a degree in nursing. Bernard died in 1983; Rosa continued to work as a nursing assistant in Oshkosh until her retirement in 1994.

5

Greece and Hungary

THE HOLOCAUST reached southeastern Europe somewhat later than it did the rest of the continent. Greece remained neutral until October 28, 1940, when Italy invaded the country. The Greeks fought the Italians to a standstill until April 6, 1941, when German troops entered the fray. Greece surrendered on April 23 and was divided into three zones: Italy occupied central and southern Greece, including Athens; Germany held central Macedonia (including Salonika) and part of Thrace; and Bulgaria controlled the rest of Thrace. Until September, 1943, when Germany took over the Italian-controlled sector of Greece, Jews were able to seek refuge in Athens. After that, however, Jews in Athens and elsewhere in southern Greece were also arrested and deported to Auschwitz, where most were gassed on arrival. Ultimately, three of every four Greek Jews perished in the Holocaust.

Jews in Hungary were also protected from the Nazi regime for several years. From the time of Hitler's rise to power, Hungary forged a close but ambivalent relationship with the Nazi state: dreams of a return to the glory of the Austro-Hungarian empire coexisted with fear of a strong Germany. Beginning with the Munich agreement (1938), the two countries gradually divided up parts of Czechoslovakia, Romania, and Yugoslavia.

Hungary never wholeheartedly embraced its alliance with Germany, and Jews lived in relative safety under the Hungarian regime until March 19, 1944, when German troops occupied Hungary to prevent the latter's defection to the Allies. Hitler's Final Solution was then quickly put into effect, and 450,000 of Hungary's 650,000 Jews perished.

Salvator Moshe

Jews had lived in Greece for at least 2,000 years before the outbreak of World War II. By 1939, the country had a population of approximately 70,000 Jews, 56,000 of whom lived in Salonika, the main city

141

Salvator Moshe's
parents and sisters,
Salonika, Greece, 1935:
(l. to r.) Bella,
Leonora, Mathilde
(mother), Mary, Israel
(father), and Regina.

WHi3187/SM/1/21

and port of Macedonia, in northern Greece. Although Salonika's Jews comprised more than half the city's population, throughout the 1930s they faced growing anti-Semitism generated by a Greek fascist movement, the Ethniki Enosis Elladas (Greek National Union). The government forced stores to close on Sundays, restricted Jewish participation in the army officer corps, and required schools to emphasize Greek studies in Hebrew and Ladino schools.

Born in Salonika on September 10, 1915, Salvator Moshe was the eldest of five children and the only son. After completing his schooling, Moshe spent three years in France before coming home in 1936 to Salonika, where he worked as a shoemaker. He joined the Greek army in 1940 and fought in Albania, returning to Salonika after Germany invaded Greece. Germany installed a Greek puppet government, which implemented the Nuremberg Laws in February, 1943, segregating Jews in northern Greece into three ghettos in the vicinity of Salonika. Between March and August, 1943, the entire Jewish population of northern Greece (including Salonika) was deported, primarily to Auschwitz and Bergen-Belsen.

One day we heard Germany occupied Salonika, and everybody disappeared. They started trying to get away on their own. Now you are in the mountains. We used to meet a peasant, an Albanian, [and ask,] "How long it take from this town to this town?" The guy used to tell me, "Two hours." You have to multiply five times more because he knew his roads, he knew how to go, and you don't know. We used to go different ways. Until the time we came on the road. I dropped my gun, the only thing I had [was] a blanket. The weather started getting a little bit better. I used to sleep nights outside, where the lambs are overnight, and days I used to walk. I went in a small town I passed. It was Shabbas, and I asked where's a temple. I found the temple. At the time I was with the uniform, full of lice. I was full, full of lice. The *shammes* [sexton of the synagogue] gave me a *tallis* [prayer shawl], I wear, the service was over. After the service, I told the *shammes,* "Take the *tallis* and burn it right away because I'm full of lice." "Don't worry, my son, don't let yourself—" Nothing. He was so upset because he saw me—I couldn't see myself. I was completely full of lice. I gave the *tallis* to the man to destroy.

I started walking. Another town. Begging for a piece of bread. The farmers don't know [if] you're Jewish or not. In your uniform, you're Greek. One day I see a group of tanks, German tanks. I went to an officer, a German officer, and that day I picked some roses from someplace, some flowers I had in my hand, walking, and a blanket in one hand. I offered the roses to the German officer, and I ask where he is going, to what destination he is going with the tanks. He says, "Salonika." We are speaking French now. I couldn't speak German at the time. "Salonika. You want to go?" "Yes." He took me on top of the tank, and they left me fifty miles away from my town, because there was [a] bridge out. I walked, I am in town. Who I met before I go home? My sister, Regina. She was coming to town. Everybody thought I disappear. I never wrote letters. They had no information from me. The war was over a month, and that's what it took me, over a month, to go, because I used to walk forty miles a day, walking in the day, sleeping in the night. I told my sister, "Don't even come close. I'm going to the Turkish bath"—I knew where it was. I says, "Bring me some clothes [from] home and tell Mother I am here, I am alive. Tell everybody I am alive." I went to the Turkish bath, took off my clothes, and I told the guy to put those on the furnace—burn up. And I went home. My mother, praying and crying every day because they knew whoever didn't come got killed or disappeared. For a long time I used to sleep on the floor because [I] couldn't stand to sleep in bed because we used to sleep on the stones, whatever there was.

And the war was over, but the whole town was occupied. Every day, we used to see where the Germans, the victories. They used to occupy [town after town] from Russia, where they used to go fight with the Russians. For a year the Germans didn't do nothing to the Jewish people.

There was a lull, after the occupation, after a year, and then the Jewish stars, the Jewish star they gave to us on everything. But before the ghetto, before we had the Jewish stars, they started taking the Jewish people into forced labor. And I declared [that] I know from shoe repair. There was a Jewish man, he took some order for the Germans to work to make shoes for the officers and they were looking for professional people and I went and I worked with this man. And you couldn't even afford to buy a piece of bread what the pay was.

One day a German officer came with an interpreter, a Greek [who] was interpreting German. I was the revolutionary there. I used to tell [that] we can't work without food, we can't work with this and this, and I started talking and the German officer came to me, and he starts to put two hands to slap my face. He didn't even touch me. The man, he had the order from the Germans, he told I am the revolutionary, I am going to revolt the people not to work, and all the Germans left, the officer left, and the interpreter [stayed]. I took the guy, I hold him. I was ready to throw [him] out of the window. The other boys, they hold me [back]. I said, "You, you Jew, and you try to tell this because you want to save your life. You want to save it, why you don't see this and this and this. They are children. Why do you think he's going to support you because you took this order and you want to—"

When were you deported from Salonika?

In 1943, between March and April.

How did it happen?

Like I said before, it was organized. This section of town goes this week—and you had to go. And you stayed with the family, together, from this ghetto until the time the trains were there and the [people were] all together in one train, like sardines. The time was going and going and going. Nobody even tried to escape from the train.

How long did the trip take?

Four days, four or five days. We passed Serbia, Hungary, Czechoslovakia, Romania, and then Poland.

And when the train stopped, where were you?

In Poland, in Auschwitz.

What happened when you got off the train?

Everybody got off from the train, and then they started selecting, men in one section, women in another section. Older men in a different section. My brother-in-law, the one that's now in Israel, Maurice Moshe, was next to me and my father was next to me. Everybody was in line, and a German officer, he select—"You go there; you stay." And they took away my father. My father was not an old man, was a young man, but he had glasses. What kind of appearance they gave to him, I don't know. And the same to the end of the line. When they organized the younger people on line, up, walk our destination to Auschwitz in the camp. We left. We didn't see anymore the relatives. We didn't see where they went, what they're doing. We don't know nothing.

Just you and your brother-in-law?

My brother-in-law and I, we went to the transport. They were supposed to be *Arbeitslager* [work camps]. The younger people, they [were sent] to the work camp.

So you were separated from your mother and your sisters?

The whole family. At that point, we don't see nobody more.

Did you see any of them ever again?

No, never again, never again. No. Went in the camp. There was an interpreter, a Greek interpreter. He's says, "If anybody he had malaria in Greece"—because the Germans, they knew there was malaria disease in Greece—"they should go out. We're going to take them in the special hospitals." That was all lie. There was no truth. They go right to the gas chamber. But we don't know nothing. Everything was smooth. We didn't know what was going on. We did not know. We did not know at all what was going on. A few people tried. I'm alive myself. I didn't see nothing, and I had some people next to me, they want to go out. I said, "You stay here." But no. But a few people, they went out. What happened, we don't know.

The second step was everybody in the room take a shower. Shave hair, complete, bottom up. Men barbers—they shaved them. They shaved the whole body. And we left the clothes down—everything—and they gave us striped clothes and we went out, the jacket, the pants, and the cap.

Did they tattoo your arm?

Not yet, not yet, no. That's second, that's after. And there were dispersed in different blocks in Auschwitz. So many people in one block and so many people in another block. Somebody they used to take this group goes in this block and this group goes into another block. My block was thirteen. It was two blocks. And there was no barrack, there was a brick foundation. [I was with] my brother-in-law, always together, but we went together. In the first forty days they don't take you to work out. They call quarantine. After the forty days, they are ready to send you out to work. At that time, the first week, the first days, the tattoo came. Everybody had numbers. My number: 116520. My brother-in-law was next to me; he's got 521, one number higher than I have. Then we stay together all the time in the same block.

I was lucky; the chief from the block was a German prisoner, non-Jew, politician. Every prisoner had, as a Jew, the *Magen David* [Star of David]. The non-Jews, they had a triangle. The triangle, the different colors, was the specification for what reason he is in camp. Mine was a politician, the chief of the block, he used to be in charge of the whole block, but he's prisoner, too. He's non-Jew, he's a prisoner, he wore the same clothes we have, but his people don't go to work. . . . Any other non-Jews they wore the triangles, but with different colors, and every color is the meaning, why is the reason he's in camp. In my block the chief was a politician, against the regime. That's the reason he was in camp. For him was a young fellow from Belgium, worked for him. Work, what do you mean? Cooked for him, special organized foods, cleaned the room, shined shoes, this. There used to be like a servant, and this guy never went out for work. He used to work for him. I met this young fellow because I spoke the French language, and he took me as a helper to him. I used to help him. He was a type, he didn't like to work, and I used to do his job. The chief in charge of the block, he used to speak a few words of Spanish, and I couldn't speak German all the time and I used to speak with him a few words of Spanish, and he used to like me. And he told me, "I won't let you go out to work. You're going to stay here with me." After the time, the forty days, you had to go to work and he keep me in the block to work for him. It was against the law, but he sacrificed himself, and he hide me when a control was or something. I used to hide myself. . . . I used to collect old butt cigarettes from his pockets and give to our friends. Everybody was real happy in the morning when I used to give every day to different guys. Just a butt—they weren't even cigarettes, but the non-Jews had the right to receive packages from home. The parents sent the packages.

The time came for work, my brother-in-law went out, but he gave him a good job, something not [too dangerous]. There was different jobs to be done. But they left the camp in the morning, and evening they coming back. Every evening there used to be an *Appell* [roll call], how many went out, how many there's supposed to be coming back. If anybody is miss[ing], until they bring dead or alive, so many thousand people, they had to stand until the one person missing was inside the camp. Even if he was dead, it don't mean nothing. But the count have to be right. They used to count. Food was a bowl of soup, a liter of soup, different types of soups every day, and a small piece of bread, sometimes margarine, sometimes marmalade. This was every twenty-four hours.

Did you receive any special rations?

I used to get something, but I couldn't even eat the soup. I was happy when I used to eat a piece of dry bread or with marmalade. That was more satisfaction for me. People, they used to eat more than one liter of soup. These people got their body full of water, more liquid, and they got sick. . . . I never had more than one liter of soup. Now, my brother-in-law was happy when I used to come back from work, I used to always serve more food than anybody else. I used to help him.

How long were you in Auschwitz before they sent you to Warsaw?

Six months.

Tell me about your departure from Auschwitz.

[In August, 1943,] there came an order for so many people, the first transport to Warsaw. After the ghetto was completely destroyed, they took from Birkenau and Auschwitz, from both, only Greeks. The transport was composed only of Greek people, because we don't speak Polish and the job was in contact with the Polish civilians, and they don't want the Polish Jews [to be able to talk to people]. When the transport was organized, this man, the bookkeeper, says, "Sal, I'm going to advise

Salvator Moshe,
Maurice Moshe, and
Salomon Yeni,
Weilheim,
Germany, 1945.

WHi3187/SM/23

you something. You got a better chance to go out on this from Auschwitz to freedom than to stay here. If you want to, I can keep you here. There's no problem with me. But I'm giving you advice—go.'' And I told my brother-in-law, ''We go.'' Then we went to Warsaw. Warsaw, when we went, everyone had the wooden shoes. They echo, the wooden shoes, you can hear us, so isolated. You couldn't even see a dog, you couldn't see a cat. The whole town was destroyed completely. Every home bombed, every bit. . . . I worked outside, too, cleaning the bricks and everything.

In the destroyed ghetto area?

In the destroyed area, completely destroyed. . . . Warsaw was miserable. Warsaw was the worst, worst, worst camp. People would die every day, dying, sickness, diarrhea. They came in one day, I was working inside the shoe repair shop and I saw a big truck, we were watching out the window. They took from the—there was no hospital—barrack where the people were sick, and they had the diarrhea. When you see a man, a skeleton, was a complete skeleton, nude, was fifteen below, twenty below, outside. One guy taking the number, was standing—I noticed this—wrote the number and threw them inside like a log. I don't know how many people they took them, took them to burn. There was no crematorium there, this camp—just burn up.

The disease started to spread in camp. My brother-in-law and I, we fell with the typhoid. I had the typhoid, and my brother-in-law's brother-in-law, all three, we fell in—sick. I don't remember how long we stayed in the hospital. People used to die by drinking water, not clear water. When you have the typhoid you get thirsty—they used to go where they used to wash the pans, the dishes, the pan. Next day he was gone. Myself, I was jealous. I found this man, he died and I can't die. And I was speechless all the time. I didn't want to talk to nobody because I had gold teeth. If they found I had gold teeth, the prisoners, even Greeks or anybody, would kill me just to take the teeth and buy something. I was speechless.

After Moshe had spent ten months in Warsaw, the Nazis forced him and 4,000 other prisoners to march to Dachau, some 500 miles away in Germany, and soon thereafter sent him to a nearby forced labor camp. Days before the war's end, Moshe and other prisoners were taken to the Austrian Tyrol, where they were to be massacred; however, the U.S. Army liberated them near Seeshaupt, Germany. After the war, Moshe lived in Weilheim, Germany, before immigrating to the United States in 1949. He settled in Milwaukee, where he married Thelma Seiden in March, 1950; the couple had three children. Moshe worked in a Greek grocery and in various tanneries in Milwaukee until his retirement in December, 1980. He died on January 27, 1993.

* * * * *

Louis Koplin

Born in Nelipeno, Czechoslovakia (now Ukraine), on July 30, 1920, Louis Koplin (Ludwig Kopolowitz) was the oldest of six children. The region where Koplin grew up was known as Carpathian Ruthenia. It was part of the Austro-Hungarian empire prior to World War I and was subsequently incorporated into Czechoslovakia. The multinational population had Ruthenians, a branch of the Ukrainian people (about 50 percent), Hungarians (33 percent), and Jews (15 percent). As of 1941, the region's Jewish population had reached more than 78,000. During Koplin's childhood, his family moved to nearby Svaljava, and Koplin graduated from the Munkacs Gymnasium in 1941, two years after Hungary annexed the region. The Czech government had treated the Jews relatively well, but they were now subjected to Hungary's anti-Semitic measures, which deprived Jews of basic civil rights and subjected them to socioeconomic discrimination.

Was Svaljava rural?

No, we lived in a city, and I would say the houses were as close as they would be in a city block, except without pavement, . . . and with big backyards, and they were row streets only. In other words, the whole city was composed of one single street, but the houses were built next to each other on that row of streets, and there was no depth to those villages.

Did families have their businesses at home?

Yes. As a rule there were no shops as we know it today. I recall the tailor and I recall even the grocer, they always lived under the same roof where they plied their trades, so to speak.

Did Jews and non-Jews interact?

Only on the business level, whenever business was conducted. In terms of social contact, I would say the Jews kind of stuck with each other. I would say there was not any social interaction to the degree that you see here today.

Did you experience anti-Semitism as you were growing up?

Yes, we did, and it was quite verbal and loud. You were told that you were a dirty Jew right from the moment that you could understand. On the first opportunity you ran into anybody he let you know that you were a dirty Jew and you were different from anybody else.

Did you look different from the non-Jews?

Yes. As a rule, most Jewish kids that I knew, we wore certain distinguishable features that made us different. We were easily picked out of the crowd as being Jewish. Up to the age of fourteen or fifteen, I had side *payot*, they called it, side curls, [and] I always wore a cap or a hat, whether it was winter or summer. There was something about a Jewish kid that was different than a gentile kid, and, of course, we were easily picked out of the crowd. That, of course, made us always a much better target for abuse and whatever.

Kopolowitz family, Svaljava, Czechoslovakia, ca. 1937: (front row, l. to r.) Sara, Honey (Louis's mother), Rifka, Zalman (Louis's father), Eva; (back row, l. to r.) Bernie, Lenka, Ludwig (Louis Koplin).

WHi(X3)49516

What languages did you speak?

The language spoken at home, at least in Svaljava, was Jewish. In other words, between the family members we always spoke Yiddish. As soon as we walked out of doors, depending upon who you ran into, you had to use another one or two languages to survive, to communicate. The indigenous population was primarily Ruthenian. Ruthenian is kind of an ill-defined language consisting of Russian, Slovakian, and some other mixtures of languages which had no really an official standing at any time, at least not at that time; however, it was a language which must have come through the millennia most likely out of a combination of languages. And this language we picked up very easily, and we had no problems communicating.

But the official language in school was Czech, and there was a compulsive language. And then my parents, between each other, spoke Hungarian. This was a remnant of the Austro-Hungarian monarchy, and it was always the thing to do. I would say it was the classy language, and as you traveled south of Svaljava to Munkacs, that was predominantly a Hungarian town. So any child, in order for him to survive, had to speak at least three languages.

What kind of news did you receive about what was happening to Jews elsewhere in Europe?

All kinds of news, in terms of concentration camps and killings and economic oppression and that kind of stuff.

How did this information come to you?

By word of mouth mostly, travelers.

Did people refuse to believe that things could be so bad?

Right. Or you ignored it. Even when the transports from Slovakia later on went through Svaljava and we brought food to the station for the Slovakian Jews, we handled it as if we were on the outside of it, this is something that only happens to some other people and not yourself.

Did the people in the trains try to talk to you?

They didn't have to. You could see what was happening. We knew what was happening, but we hoped that this would not happen here, and they always told us, well, these people were really foreigners to Slovakia, they were not permanent residents, that they were recentcomers. There was always explanations. That this would not happen to the permanent population. And then there was no choice, there was no escape. You always can put yourself in a defensive frame of mind if you have no choice. There was nothing you could do about it in any given stage. If I recall, my father could never, under any circumstances, even if he had decided to move his family away from Europe, he could not scrape together enough money to put us all on a train and to get us to a certain destination. It was just beyond his ability to do so, and so it was of the whole community's.

You didn't even consider moving away?

There was no escape. I mean we just take it as things come.

Did anti-Semitism increase when the Hungarians occupied the area?

Oh God. First thing they did was that they had to set up conditions under which a Jew could continue to stay in Hungary, to qualify for Hungarian citizenship. One of the conditions was that you must have lived within the Austro-Hungarian monarchy border—I don't recall whether it was a hundred years or something. I suspect it was about a hundred years, if I recall. In other words, you had to have lived or some of your ancestors must have lived within that given area since 1850. And in order to prove that, that was quite a job and that's what I did, as a matter of fact. I traveled throughout the mountains to seek out some kind of proof, whether it was in form of a birth certificate or a real estate transaction or a deed or anything like that that would prove that my ancestors, either my great-grandfather or somebody, lived there at that time, which, by the way, I successfully did find. It was a matter of a deed of some sort, deed transaction. . . . It took about a year, but by that time I already was taken into slave labor. I remember my father writing to me that they got the citizenship while I was already in slave labor.

What would the consequences have been if you couldn't find proof of citizenship?

The alternative was, for sure, death, so to speak. Because what they did is they took you and just put you across the border and abandoned you. And, of course, across the border you were also a foreign element. You were just destroyed, that's all.

> Although the Hungarian government did not take overt action against the Jews of the region, Jewish males were drafted and sent to the Russian front to dig trenches soon after the German invasion of Russia in June, 1941. Jews remained relatively safe, however, until Germany occupied Hungary. Only 20 percent of Carpathian Ruthenia's Jewish population survived the war.

In the beginning of the Hungarian occupation, the rules applying to Jews were the same as applying to the rest of the population in terms of military induction. The only difference was that if inducted the Jews were taken to nonmilitary service, such as slave labor or paramilitary, and the gentiles, of course, went into military service. In 1940 I was taken in for a medical examination, and I did not pass it because I was underweight, undernourished, under whatever have you, and then in 1941 I successfully passed the examination.

Were you any heavier than you had been in 1940?

Not really. Not, because we'd worked at it very hard not to reach a certain whatever health status. But they inducted me [anyway]. I was taken to

Komarom, which was at least a thousand kilometers away. It's on the Danube, it's west of Budapest. It was a half-Czech, half-Hungarian city. It's known as Komarno under the Czechs, it's known as Komarom under the Hungarians, and I stayed there from 1941 until 1944.

I was lucky enough to have stayed there for one reason and that is I was chosen to become a shoemaker. On the first day of our induction they lined up at least 2,000 of us and I remember the commander, who was marching in front of the line, said, "All shoemakers, one step forward." There must have been a thousand shoemakers that could have stepped forward, and by the grace of God he stopped next to me and he says, "One step out," and about three or four of us were chosen and that provided a certain security for the next three years.

Were you singled out as Jews?

Oh yes, oh sure.

How?

First of all, the uniforms that were given to us. The uniform consisted of a yellow band and military cap—that was the only uniform a Jew was given, while the gentiles were given full uniforms, with weapons and everything. And from then on, for the duration of the next four years, I was never allowed to take off my band under the threat of whatever military punishment there was.

Could you describe a typical day there?

Now, remember that my situation was not a representative situation of what it meant to be a slave laborer. Mine was only the slave labor in terms that I was confined to stay there. Otherwise things were not very unpleasant. I got up in the morning, they served us breakfast, which was in a military fashion. You lined up with your can or whatever, that container that they put food in, and we went into our labor area, where we sat down at stools like my father used to do and then we repair worked from eight or nine o'clock until noon and then we were fed lunch—the same way as any other military.

By the way, this was a big headquarters, military headquarters, this particular compound served as. But it just so happened that this military headquarters handled only Jewish affairs. So all the inductees from large areas, from all over the country, came into this. So what I was witnessing there was the bringing and gathering of all those people and then shipping them out. This was going on day in and day out, week and week out. So I saw tens of thousands of them coming and going all the time. I eventually ran into people who came from my hometown and I was able to help some of them, getting them extra food which I had access to, and what have you.

How did you come to leave Komarom?

In [March,] 1944, Horthy,[1] who was the head of the state, realized that this is a losing battle, and he resigned and wanted to get out of the war, which the Germans prevented him from doing. They arrested him, but they set up their own government, which was the Green Cross. The Hungarian Fascist party took over, and that day when this happened, an order came into the camp that all who wish to leave the camp may do so. They were free to go. Also, in the same time, rumors were spread that if we were able to get to Budapest, we could pick up some international passports, such as Swedish, Swiss, and papal passports. And with these passports in possession, we could possibly either be able to live in Budapest or be able to leave Hungary. I have no idea how that was contemplated, but anyway, there was the whole idea. So all of us picked up our belongings, whatever we had, got on a train, and went to Budapest.

How could you leave the camp?

It was just abandoned. All the military just left. The whole thing just dismantled because there was a complete breakdown of government control. In other words, we thought this is it, this is the end. Little did we know that Germany, of course, would not just stand by and do nothing. So we left for Budapest and got to Budapest. We were told, I don't know who even told us but it must be some of the Jewish fellows who got hold of some information [that] said we should go to a certain place, which we did, and if I recall, I was given a Swedish passport.

But of course it was of no avail because the next day walking on the street we were questioned by roaming patrols and what have you and asked for identification. As soon as they saw that this identification was

---

[1] Miklos Horthy (1868–1957) served as regent of Hungary, 1920–1944. Under his leadership, Hungary allied itself with Germany during World War II.

of questionable origin, they arrested us, and they took us all, by the thousands, because they were coming from all over, which must have been in the same situation as I was, because many camps all over the area must have been abandoned. They rounded us up into some military compound in Budapest, and they marched us to the railroad stations and loaded us up into cattle cars and they shipped us to Austria.

What was Budapest like when you arrived there?

There was complete chaos. I had no idea what was happening. It was a feeling of elation, yet there was a feeling of fear as to what is going to be, because it was very obvious that this is not the end of it, it cannot be the end of it. There were too many military around. We didn't know what was happening, and this is exactly what happened. Out of nowhere we were just arrested and all I could see is thousands and thousands and thousands of us being herded into trains. I mean endless, endless, endless transports. Jewish transports were being shipped.

Did you consider going back to Svaljava?

No, not at that time, because I already knew at that time that there were problems at home. Already heard that they were already rounding them up because the Russians were threatening, and the Germans already were there at the time. I had some communications from my parents, desperate communications. They felt that this is the end, something terrible is going to happen. They described an event that happened to them during Passover, during the Passover meal. They forced them to take in some German officers for lodging. I don't know how in the world there was room for anything like this, but anyway they had one or two German officers as lodgers. And one of them—this is the oddest thing—one of them participated in the services, a German officer, and they couldn't figure out why he cried throughout the service. They suspected he may have had some Jewish background because he participated in the seder services. I knew this letter very vividly. This was the last communication that I had.

When did you learn what had happened to your family?

Not until after the war. I had no idea what happened. But by that time my situation changed for the worse and there was no way for me to find out, and it was a matter of life or death for me, from day to day existence.

What happened after the train arrived in Austria?

They let us out on the Austria-Hungarian border, . . . and then the next day they separated again, created groups, and we were sent to a tent camp. And from there we were sent every morning out to work. And the work that was done was digging military ditches for [use] against the Russians—military enforcements. And we did that from the end of summer, somehow around there, I don't recall exactly when I got there, until about January or February of 1945.

What kind of rations did you receive?

One soup a day, that was it, once a day. If you're lucky enough to get to the beginning of the line, you'd still get some solid pieces in there. If you came to the end of the line, it was all just water or sometimes nothing was left. Fortunately, I was in prime shape when I started this ordeal, and . . . I went out to work a few times but then I managed to finagle a job that I didn't have to go out, that I worked right on the premises. That provided a certain amount of protection for me, too.

What did you do?

I don't even recall. But all I know that I did not have to go out. I did some work in the camp. I don't even remember what. All I know that the death rate was frightening and every other day or so they asked for volunteers to remove the dead bodies. I managed to avoid that somehow. Somehow they didn't notice me, or I was too small. I managed to hide so they didn't pick me to do it. Because what it meant really was every other day or every third day to load those bodies up into a truck or a wagon to haul them away because all the bodies were dumped into one tent. When it filled up, then they just hauled them away. The death rate was frightening.

   We had very little protection from the elements there. It was in a tent situation. When it snowed, it snowed and then it melted the water you were sleeping practically under water. I think I had very good shoes and I must have had a good coat that I must have been protected, because I never got sick. Most of them got sick and, of course, died, and malnutrition, disease, what have you. They seemed to have kept up the count by bringing in fresh people to replace the dead ones, but this really was the first time when I started seeing what this was all about, what was happening to the Jews for the past three-four years. I had no idea. This is what you heard about, but I never witnessed it.

Was it a terrible shock for you?

It is not a matter of shock, because it's a matter of resignation. It's a matter of take it and make the best of it—survive. I never made an issue of anything. In other words, if you did that, then that was the end. Somehow I managed to survive. Maybe I managed to blot out what happened there because this was really a very bad experience. . . . Like you ask me what did I do, and I don't have [any] recollection of what I did. How can you blot out three-four months or whatever? All I remember is certain times that I went out to work and I knew that I could not survive that ordeal day in, day out. And something happened that I didn't have to go out. What happened, I don't recall.

I know one thing—that there was some women there. There was a young lady who was, I think, attractive, whatever recollection I have. She caught the attention of the commander, and he took her into his quarters. Nobody questioned as to what she did or what she didn't do, but I know one thing: with regularity, she brought me food. I got to know her, and something happened between us that she felt she ought to protect me, and I remember her very distinctly meeting me regularly every day and bringing me a piece of bread, a piece of meat, I recall, fruit—things that were very sustaining in terms of life. And this was going on for quite some time.

What happened in February, 1945?

Then the Russians occupied Budapest. They started threatening the Austrian-Hungarian front. They picked us up and set us out in a death march, which I didn't know what the march was, but I remember the snow started melting, and we got on the road. That's all I remember. We started marching, and the march never ended.

How many people were there?

We started out just the people that were in this camp. We marched for half a day and other people joined us, and more people joined us and more people joined us. And we started marching. We went by way of Vienna, so I knew we were marching west. And we went through the whole Austrian Alps and it started out somewhere around February or March. Really, these dates are completely not clear. And groups were joining us from all over.

How long did you march each day? When and where did you sleep?

We marched until sundown, and then they said, "Stop." And we stopped, wherever we stopped, and wherever you were you lied down, and you slept. . . .

I remember seeing the first sight of the Alps and it was the most magnificent view. It was unbelievable how beautiful it was. And I remember marching next to my fellow marcher and I looked up at him and I said, "Look how beautiful this is." He looks back up at me and says, "You must be insane." So it must have been something that my attitude was such that I still saw hope, I still saw beauty. This one comment I'll never forget. And of course he had no chance for survival.

Did you have any contact with the villagers whom you passed?

The people never helped. Once in a while the guard, who happened to march with you—most of them were the old guards, they didn't use the real soldiers, they used only older people—and you befriended the man and he was no fool. He saw what was going on. So he was being fed, so he had a hot potato or something, a boiled potato. He gave you half a potato . . . and that half potato carried you over the next twenty-four hours.

> The march, during which more than 95 percent of the prisoners died, covered more than 300 miles and ended at Mauthausen, a concentration camp in Austria. Six weeks later, the Nazi guards fled the camp, which was liberated within a few days by the U.S. Army. For several months Louis worked for American Jewish relief agencies and traveled throughout Europe searching for family members.

How did you find your brother?

[My brother and I] practically chased each other all over Europe. Whatever town we came to, I heard about him being in a particular city. By the time I got there, of course he was gone. But he heard the same way about me and of course by the time he got after me, he was gone. But eventually we did meet up at home, and that is in our own home

WHi3187/KP/1/2

*Louis Koplin (standing, far left) with other relief workers,
Munich, Germany, 1946.*

birthplace. I found out about that also by hearsay, by somebody telling
me, "He is home. If you go there right now, you'll find him."

This was in Nelipeno?

And then this was in Nelipeno. And I remember, I don't know how it
happened, because we obviously did not know, there was no such
communication possible for us to let each other know that we were
coming. I was coming from the direction of Svaljava, which is in the
south of that small town, and as I approached the last little hill, after
which you approached that small village, . . . there he appeared beyond
the horizon coming toward me. I'll never forget that scene. He must
have seen me in the same time, and we both ran toward each other, and
of course it was a very nice event, which I don't think we'll ever forget.

How did you find out that your sister was alive?

Traveling between Prague and Budapest on one of the trips, getting into
one of those cabins, I was trying to sit down on one of those benches.
The bench seemed to have been very muddy, and on the floor there was

a piece of newspaper. I picked up the piece of newspaper in order to wipe off the bench, and as I held the newspaper in my hand, I suddenly noticed a list of names, with a heading saying that the following persons were taken to Sweden by the Red Cross. There was my sister's name, practically either the second or the third name on top of the list. I got off at the next station, because I knew Budapest could not provide any communications because it was not a liberated city; it was an occupied city, very badly destroyed. I got on a train going the other way, got to Prague, sent her a telegram, and within twenty-four hours we were in communication with each other. That's how I found out about my sister.

How did you find out what had happened to the rest of your family?

In one of the lines waiting to be fed I met someone who told me that my father had died about a week after liberation. About the rest of my family I found out from my sister, who actually witnessed most of it. She witnessed the separations—of course, so did my brother—the separation from each other of my mother and the youngest two children. She managed to hold on to Rifka, who was the third oldest, and she held on to her for quite some time until finally she could not keep her fed enough to qualify for work. One day they just grabbed her away and that was it.

My brother was with my father for a long period of time in Auschwitz. Then they were both transferred to Buchenwald, and there again they took care of each other as long as they could. Eventually they got separated, even though my brother hoped that [my father] would be all right, but I guess he didn't make it.

I was the only one who was alone, away, the farthest, left home first, and all I know is that my brother tells me and my sister tells me, she says that even on the way to Auschwitz, in the crowded train, my mother always kept saying, "I wonder how Dudi is doing." Even then, when she saw that she had enough reason to worry about the immediate people who were with her, [she] kept wondering what my fate was at the time.

And I think I mentioned to you before that there was one thing I always hoped: I kind of wished and secretly hoped that I would not run into anybody during the death march because survival by itself, of one's own person, was so overwhelming that to worry about another person would have made the job an impossibility. It was always much harder for people to survive who were with their close ones.

Koplin fled Czechoslovakia in April, 1946, and worked for the American Jewish Joint Distribution Committee while in a displaced persons camp in Germany. He came to the United States the following year and enrolled at the University of Wisconsin in Madison in September, 1947, receiving a degree in pharmacy in 1951. After graduating, he moved to Milwaukee, where he married Lorraine Eder in 1954; the couple subsequently had three children. Koplin opened his own pharmacy in Milwaukee in 1957, operating it until his retirement in 1992. Lorraine Koplin died in 1992.

* * * * *

Magda Moses Herzberger

Born in Cluj, Romania (Transylvania), on February 20, 1926, Magda Moses was an only child. By 1940, Transylvania had a population of approximately 200,000 Jews, more than 160,000 of them in the northern part of the region, which was annexed by Hungary on August 30, 1940. Life for Cluj's nearly 17,000 Jews subsequently worsened, and the Moses family was forced to move into a small apartment. When Germany occupied Hungary in March, 1944, the status of Jews deteriorated even further, and by May of that year the Jews of Cluj and outlying areas were enclosed in a ghetto. Within a month the ghetto was liquidated, and the Moses family was sent to Auschwitz. Only a third of the ghetto's inhabitants survived the war.

WHi3187/HZB/2/21

Magda Moses with her parents, Herman and Serena, Cluj, Romania, ca. 1931.

We realized in what circumstances we were when we were taken into the cattle wagons, and there were huge lines, many people. It was like a madhouse at the cattle wagons. Pushed into those wagons, so many we could hardly move, . . . and they were dark inside. Then they closed the door, that hard steel door, and they locked us from outside. We didn't get any food, we didn't get any drink, nothing. I remember after they locked the doors, my father said, "We were fools." He said, "We are trapped." And it was too late to escape. We realized and he realized and everyone realized that we were trapped. The first time that we had no hope for better, because we did not receive humane treatment. And can you imagine when somebody had to use the restroom? There was no restroom, we had to do everything there in that wagon, and the men had to turn away, and you had to do everything. [The train ride lasted] three days and three nights, [and during this time] they didn't let us out. . . . We thought that we are going to be taken and annihilated. Otherwise why would you treat a person like that? We knew that we were not going to go into the place where we were promised to go. . . .

I remember as we were going, riding the train, we were with so many you had to sleep just like sardines, next to each other, and I was sleeping, and I could feel the tears. One thing which remains, that painful sensation just like it would be now. I could feel the tears, the warm tears, of my father falling on me, and I was silent. He was a very proud, controlled man, and I was silent. But I could feel that pain, and he just said, "It's too late, it's too late for everything." We were trapped. He had a bad premonition at that point. He had a bad premonition when we parted. When we were in the train he talked to me as [if] he would know that he might not return. He was hoping that the young people maybe get better treatment. But his trust was really shattered.

Then when we arrived, it was horrible. Some were exhausted; others cried. There was somebody having a nervous breakdown there. We were uncombed and unkempt and dirty and feeling like a cattle. That's the way we arrived to Auschwitz. First thing, I can never forget that feeling, when the train stopped and everything was silent, and it's just like in those moments you know something is going to happen and you don't know what exactly it's going to be. And then soon after, you hear the voices of the German soldiers and boom, [the door of the wagon was] opened with force. Everything was [done] in a shocking way. Nothing was done gently. But in the moment that [the doors] were opened, there came in the violence. The monster of hatred and violence was coming after us. Then we heard the voices of the soldiers and they came in, and they were really treating us brutally, pushing us, coming with the

short rubber sticks. We had to go fast. If you didn't get out fast from
that wagon, you got hit in the back. And we had to leave everything
inside, and then you got out of the wagon, and the first thing that struck
us [was] the huge flames belching from big chimneys. We could see
them back in the distance. But it was such a strange sickening odor of
burning flesh. We did not know what that was at that time. I had no
idea that those were the furnaces, because no one could imagine such
a thing.

And then right there, you see the German officials and you had to
form rows of five and then they look at you, they point you left, right,
left, right, and you had horrible scenes. Children being snatched, babies
from their mothers, the mothers were running crazily after them and
then you see the mothers who run crazily after their children [being taken
to the gas chambers with their children]. When the men were separated
from the women and families separated, there was a painful cry. People
were running, there were shots in the air, then people were beaten up.
I was so shocked that in the first moment I could not imagine that this
is true. I thought I must be dreaming, this cannot happen to me. And
you know in those few minutes things happened fast. Many of my family
members were pointed to the left, all the little children in our family.
All the uncles and aunts of my mother's were pointed to the left. We
didn't know at that time where they go.

The ambulances came, with red cross, all the older people, all the
invalids or people who were sick were taken in. The guards were lying
to us, "They will be taken to the hospital." Little did they know that
they are going to be taken right to the gas chambers. So they looked
for help, they mounted those trucks, [and] you never have seen them
again. And then within minutes I was all by myself. I can never forget
that moment. I looked and I was separated from my family. There I was,
standing with strangers and I was looking for a familiar face, and I have
seen my father walking with my uncle. I looked back, there they were.
I never have seen them again. That was the last glimpse I had of them.
And then, what happened after that? After that, the trains left.

When we were separated and already I was there by myself, [I started
paying] attention to my surroundings, because in those few moments
[at the beginning] I couldn't even pay attention to my surroundings or
where I was because there were so many painful things happening. Then
I paid attention, and I have seen the barbed-wire fence of Auschwitz.
There were posts connected with wire, and at the top of each post there
were huge lamps projected at you, like a big watching eye, peering at
you at all times. And then I have seen people, women, coming to the

fence, begging for food. They looked insane. I thought that this was the insane asylum, I really did. They were shaved, in rags, looking terrible; they looked like insane people, and I had no idea that within a few minutes I would be there just like them. . . .

And then the first thing what we did we had to strip naked in the front of the shaving room and we had to leave everything behind. I was eighteen years old. I don't think anyone had seen me naked except my mother. And I remember the shame I felt. I remember I was hiding my breasts. We were naked and the German soldiers were lined up and laughing at us. Can you imagine that? I was hiding between the other women, I was covering my breasts. I can never forget that. I felt so terribly humiliated. . . . Not enough you march naked, but they laugh at you.

And then, the shaving room, where they shaved you in all your places. First they shaved our heads. I had long hair, I had thick braids. I didn't cut my hair since the first elementary grade. And then I could see—I can see now even—I go back in time, I go through terrible emotions right now because I remember the SS woman, the first time I have seen an SS woman. They were just as cruel and heartless as the men, and she was there in the shaving room, courted by an SS guard, and they were laughing and making jokes. But I came there and then she put the shears and I was pleading, "Leave me please just a little hair." I was so naive, so young. And she was laughing with her boyfriend. There I stood naked, and they [were] laughing, and she goes for the shears and shaves my whole head. I was so horrified, I was in shock. In the first hour in Auschwitz, I was in shock. I couldn't cry, I couldn't think this through. I thought that I'm going through a nightmare and soon I will wake up. . . . Finally, I could hear the little noise and I glimpsed back—you were not even allowed to move this way or this way—and I glimpsed back and I can never forget that my whole braid, my beautiful long hair, was in one piece on the ground. I was shocked, like you pause a moment, like you feel paralyzed. You don't even want to go. It's like a feeling that you don't want to go a step further.

And then I felt a brutal blow in my back, a guard hitting my bare flesh with that little rubber stick and pushing me toward the shower room. And then the shower room, pushed, fast, fast, fast. [We were] brutally treated. And then out from the shower room, [we entered a dressing room, where they threw] you some rags, really. All the good things were taken. I got a long, dark blue, dress down to [my ankles], twice as big [as needed]. No underwear, nothing, just that thing. It [looked] like a sack, and then I got the wrong shoes, high shoes, [with an] orthopedic [insert]. I could hardly walk with it. And then from there they pushed you into the paint room. . . . The back [of the dress] was painted with a red stripe so that if you try to escape they can see you from far, the red strip of paint. And then they pushed you out from that room, and I was so horrified, I came out and I was still in a daze. . . .

And then finally we got to the barracks, and I have seen the barracks [and] my fellow prisoners eating grass. We were pushed in that huge barrack, 500 people. We had nothing in the barracks. There were no more bunks. Other barracks had just pieces of wood where many people were lying. But we had nothing, just the barren floor of that huge barrack, and I tell you we had to sleep crouched, like when you are an embryo. That's the way we had to sleep through the night. And then five people got one blanket. . . . In that moment I think I have seen something that really shook me as a person. People were fighting for the blanket. Everyone wanted that same blanket. I still was not myself. We got no food, nothing, until the morning, when we had black coffee. [At the end of my first day in Auschwitz], I lay down [in my barrack], gradually it dawned on me that [all the terrible experiences] were real. There were hours and hours passing by. [Everything] was real. . . . I pinched myself until it hurt. I hurt myself until I felt a sharp pain, and I told myself, "I feel pain. This is real. It's not imaginary. It's not a dream." . . . I started crying and crying and crying. All this was coming out, out, out, and finally I fell asleep. And when I fell asleep I was at home, and I was combing my long hair. Because that was a terrible shock. I was dreaming with my hair.

I must have slept a while and then it was around four o'clock, when suddenly out of that dream I heard the word—it was dark in the barrack—I heard "Heraus, heraus! [Get out, get out!]" and just like a raid coming in, like a madhouse, the guards coming in, the SS, with the little rubber sticks, taking us out for *Appell* [roll call], to count us, to see if everyone is there, if no one escaped, who is alive and who is dead. So we had to get out. It was cold, we had no underwear. That was my first morning in Auschwitz, standing in line for hours and hours until they counted us. After a while you really got tired, because you were already emotionally exhausted. So some [people] started slumping a little. There came the guard, hitting you in the face. You had to stand up. You [slump] twice, or three times, you are slapped, you are punished. Because two people in our lines were slacking, three times we were punished and we had to kneel in clay and in stone for hours. There was a physician next to me who during the night tore up a little piece from her blanket because she was cold, and put it around her breast. While we were kneeling one of the SS women observed that she is hiding something, and she took [the little piece of blanket from] her and she was slapping and slapping and slapping her. And I remember her face was getting red and red and she just had to stand [there getting slapped]. . . . After a while she just couldn't take it. She got up like in a frenzy, she started beating the SS woman. They took her away. We never have seen her. I realized what happens to you if you just show any protest. That was my first morning in Auschwitz.

During her six weeks in Auschwitz, Moses encountered a young woman whom she had befriended years before in school.

When I was in the first grade, there were two girls in the classroom, and they were really very poor. It was customary there to bring something at ten o'clock, a little snack, and then we got milk in school. My mother always prepared me a little snack, because in the morning we usually did not eat very much—I would only drink a little coffee and have a crescent [roll]. Then at ten o'clock the children had recess and then we would eat. . . . One day I was just about biting into my little snack when suddenly my eyes fell on these two girls, and I could see two eyes staring at me. They were looking [me intensely]. In that moment that bite got caught in my throat. I just couldn't swallow it, and I thought, "Well, at home I'm going to get a good meal, and I'm not sure what these girls are going to get." So I gave them my bread and I would have some sandwich, some meat or something, egg in it, and then I would come home and I would feel ravenous, I would eat everything. . . . That was my little secret for a while. And then one day my mother came to me and she said, "You have to tell me the truth. What do you do with your snack?" And then I confessed it to her. My mother said, "Why did you have to wait so long? From now on you will take [something] every day for those girls." So she packed [a snack] every single day for those girls.

Now, this time passed and I was in the camps and a strange thing happened. One of the girls was in Auschwitz, in the same barrack with me, and I was very pleased to see her. . . . One night I woke up with such a heavy feeling and a terrible depression descended upon me, and [for the] first time maybe I was questioning if it's worthwhile really to survive, if it's a possibility to escape and if it's worth to fight for. And I thought, "Well, I'm going to find out if I go out and look at the wire, see if I can touch it or not and end my life." . . . [I left the barrack,] and I was standing there and thinking—to touch it or not to. I really was pondering with the question, to be or not to be. As I was thinking, suddenly I heard somebody coming, footsteps, and somebody putting a hand on my shoulder. And who do you think it was? My friend. She said, "Magda, what are you doing here? What kind of thoughts do you have? I woke up and I have seen you crawling and I was worried for you. Don't you know that you are the only child and what are you going to do to your parents? What happened to you? Did you give up fighting?" And she was standing [there]. Finally we ended up both crying. But she never forgot that I helped her, and she had the possibility now to help me. We went back together. That was the last time I was thinking of doing something like that.

I was taken to Bergen-Belsen then, and I never have seen her after that, and I didn't know what happened to her. And my mother said one day she [was shopping] in Tel Aviv [after the war] . . . and she heard somebody calling her name. [The girl] recognized her. She was grateful to her. Something like that you don't forget. And she was telling my mother about this night. This is the mitzvah. I think that what you give, you get it back.

WHi3187/HZB/1/14

Magda and Eugene Herzberger at the time of their wedding, Cluj, Romania, November, 1946.

After six weeks in Auschwitz, Moses was moved to Bremen, Germany, where she endured forced labor. In March, 1945, she and the other surviving prisoners were marched about twenty miles to the Bergen-Belsen concentration camp, where she was liberated by British troops three weeks later. She returned to Cluj in late 1945 and was reunited with her mother. In April, 1946, Magda Moses began medical school, where she met Eugene Herzberger, whom she married in November of that year. The Herzbergers and Magda's mother fled Romania in 1947 with 16,000 other Jews and lived on the island of Cyprus and in Israel before immigrating to the United States in 1957. The couple and their two children settled in Monroe, Wisconsin, where Eugene Herzberger worked as a neurosurgeon. They moved to Dubuque, Iowa, in 1976 and retired to Arizona in 1994. Magda's mother lived with the Herzbergers until her death in 1994. Magda Herzberger has spoken extensively on her Holocaust experiences and has published a memoir, *Eyewitness to Holocaust* (Mattoon, Illinois, 1985), and a volume of Holocaust poetry, *Waltz of the Shadows* (New York, 1983). She has also composed musical pieces on the subject.

Index

American Jewish Joint Distribution Committee, 162

Amsterdam, The Netherlands, 29, 44-58

Anti-Semitism: in Czechoslovakia, 150-151; in Greece, 142; in Hungary, 149, 152-153; in Lithuania, 75; in the Netherlands, 30, 32, 44-45, 50-52; in Poland, 72, 83-84, 114-115, 122-123

Appleton, Wisconsin, 122

Auschwitz concentration camp, vii, 30, 108-112, 129-134, 141, 142, 144-148, 161, 162, 163-169

Austria, 1-2, 22, 156, 157-159

Bader, Aron, 58

Bader, Flora Melkman van Brink Hony, 44-58

Badoglio, Pietro, 70, 70n

Baras, Edward, 86, 92-93

Baras, Ellen, 93

Baras, Lucy Rothstein, 80-93

Baras, Victor, 92

Belorussia, 72

Bergen-Belsen concentration camp, 142, 168, 169

Bergsma family, 52

Berlin, Germany: forced labor in, 134-137; hiding in, 12-22; *Kristallnacht* in, 2-4

Bernadotte, Folke, 138-139, 138n

Birkenau concentration camp, 109, 110, 147. *See also* Auschwitz concentration camp

Blonk, ———, 54-55

Bombings, 24-27, 136-137

Buchenwald concentration camp, 29, 119-121, 161

Budapest, Hungary, 155-156

Bulgaria, 141

Campagna, Italy, 64-65

Canada, 43

China, vii, 22-28, 63

Clothing: in Auschwitz, 165-166; in hiding in Polish forest, 90

Colditz, Germany, 121

Concentration camps: Auschwitz, vii, 30, 108-112, 129-134, 141, 142, 144-148, 161, 162, 163-168; Bergen-Belsen, 142, 168, 169; Birkenau, 109, 110, 147; Buchenwald, 119-121, 161; Czestochowa, 118-119; Dachau, vii, 78, 112, 149; Ferramonte, 65, 66-70; in Italy, 59; knowledge of during the war, 46, 49, 55-56; Majdanek, 107-108; Mauthausen, 50, 159;

Neuengamme, 58; Oranienburg-Sachsenhausen, 6-10, 112; Sobibór, 30; Theresienstadt, 121; Treblinka, 117; Vught, 30; Westerbork, 30

Czechoslovakia, 141, 149-162

Czestochowa concentration camp, 118-119

Dachau concentration camp, vii, 78, 112, 149

Dalsine family, 33-37

Death camps. *See* Concentration camps

Death march, 149, 158-159

Delavan, Wisconsin, 122

DeLevie, Deena, 44

DeLevie, Edith, 30-44

DeLevie, Herb, 30-44

DeLevie, Hertha, 30-44

DeLevie, Monica Freund-Fasslicht, 44

DeLevie, Nathan, 30-44

Denmark, 139-140

Deutschkron, Erich, 14, 18

Deutschkron, Eva Lauffer, 12-22

Deutschkron, Martin, 12-22

Displaced persons (DP) camps, 92-93

Dolle Dinsdag (Crazy Tuesday), 58, 58n

Dollfuss, Engelbert, 63, 63n

Drente family, 33, 37-38

Education: in hiding, 40-41; in prewar Poland, 82-83

Ellis Island, 10-12

England. *See* Great Britain

Estonia, 72

Ethniki Enosis Elladas (Greek National Union), 142

Eyewitness to Holocaust (Magda Herzberger), 169

Ferramonte concentration camp, 66-70

Food: in Auschwitz, 130, 147; in Austrian prison camp, 157; in DP camps, 93; in Italian concentration camps, 64, 67; in Lodz ghetto, 126; in the Netherlands, 35, 36; while hiding in Polish forest, 88-89

Forced labor, 117-118, 121, 134-137, 154

Frank, Anne, 30, 53

Friedlander, Professor, 5

Gas chambers, 107-108, 131

Gebhardt, Franz Erich, 15, 17, 19